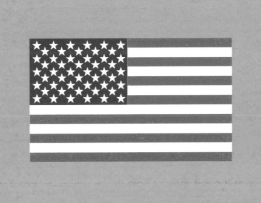

# US

**PHILIP JODIDIO**

# ARCHITECTURE IN THE UNITED STATES

**TASCHEN**

HONG KONG KÖLN LONDON LOS ANGELES MADRID PARIS TOKYO

#3

#4
#10

#8
#12

#6

9/14 #

#16

#2

#17

#1/4/9

#5

#6

#11

#11

#13

#15

#10

# INTRODUCTION

## STAIRWAY TO HEAVEN

"Change is the one immutable circumstance found in landscape. But the changes all speak or sing in unison of cosmic law, itself a nobler form of change. These cosmic laws are the physical laws of all man-built structures as well as the laws of the landscape. Man takes a positive hand in creation whenever he puts a building upon the earth beneath the sun. If he has a birthright at all, it must consist in this: that he, too, is no less a feature of the landscape than the rocks, trees, bears, or bees that nature to which he owes his being. Continuously, nature shows him the science of her remarkable economy of structure in mineral and vegetable constructions to go with the unspoiled character everywhere apparent in her forms."
**FRANK LLOYD WRIGHT, The Future of Architecture**[1]

The words of Frank Lloyd Wright, written near the end of his long career, speak of buildings inevitably linked to nature. Wright's own conception of "organic" architecture surely had its followers in the United States and elsewhere, but the contemporary situation, the very future that Wright spoke of, seems more distant from the precepts of the greatest of America's 20th-century architects than he might have hoped. The format and size of this book do not allow it to pretend to be a complete overview of architecture in the United States. Rather a certain number of recent highlights have been selected, without regard for the defense of a particular style. The selected projects and architects range from the celebrated (Frank O. Gehry) to the less well known (Michael Jantzen) with a gamut of figures in between who have each, in their own way, marked the architectural scene. There are Pritzker Prize winners (Gehry, Meier, and Thom Mayne of Morphosis), established innovators like Eric Owen Moss, or Steven Holl. They are based in the East (Williams & Tsien, James S. Polshek), the West (Wes Jones, Boora, or Antoine Predock), or the South (Rural Studio). There are innovators who work at the edge, between the virtual and the real, like Asymptote and Jantzen, or rising stars like Diller Scofidio + Renfro and LTL Lewis.Tsurumaki.Lewis. The point of this enumeration is to emphasize the variety present in this selection, which can serve at the very least as an exciting introduction to a world that seems to have left behind not only Wright, but also Gropius and Mies.

## SEX AND THE CITY

Since their first appearance on the architectural scene, with their 1988 prize-winning commission for the Los Angeles West Coast Gateway, Lise Anne Couture and Hani Rashid of Asymptote have been stretching the limits of contemporary architecture through a combination of imagined environments, such as their proposals for a virtual trading floor for the New York Stock Exchange, or the Guggenheim Virtual Museum, and actual construction. Their Carlos Miele Flagship Store on West 14th Street in Manhattan ( 2002–03) combines a keen sense of space and a wrap-around environment in high-gloss epoxy or stretched PVC rubber. Having long been interested in objects, Hani Rashid, who is the brother of noted designer Karim Rashid, is taking the plunge into the active creation of office objects for

Alessi. Asymptote was just completing the new flagship store for Alessi in New York when this book went to press. Hani Rashid's combination of virtual environments, actual architecture, and objects is certainly very much in the mood of the moment. Art and architecture are often hard to completely separate, and design, too, is taking the road of an increasing integration into the architectural environment. This movement, supported by technological advances, is not using the same sort of utopian framework that inspired the Bauhaus idea of the gesamtkunstwerk, but it might well go in the same direction as that first imagined in Germany.

An artistic approach has in fact become a hallmark of the work of many American architects, not least among them the New York-based Steven Holl. His process inevitably begins with watercolor renderings, meticulously ordered in albums that he keeps in his office. His project featured here, the Turbulence House, was designed for the sculptor Richard Tuttle for a site in New Mexico. Despite its beginnings in the sensitive drawings of Steven Holl, this irregularly shaped residence was built using parametric design and an unusual aluminum skin. Where it might have been expected that computers would serve mainly to develop new, mathematically morphed forms, Holl's office uses them instead to create the 3-D models required for the manufacture of an essentially artistic conception. Another unusual aspect of the Turbulence House is that it has an exact twin, in a sculpture park in Schio, Italy, near Vicenza.

Holl's recently completed Swiss Residence in Washington D.C. (with Rüssli Architects), is a case of exemplary collaboration between American and European firms. Strict and yet sufficiently complex to allow Holl to make his trademark use of light and subtle color, the Residence is at once modest in good Swiss tradition and sufficiently ample to allow the Embassy to receive two hundred guests or more at a time. In this instance, Steven Holl demonstrates that the repercussions of Modernism and its adaptation to today's circumstances is very much part of American architecture. His work is both original and yet firmly rooted in site and function.

Another New York firm, Diller Scofidio + Renfro, has long participated in the design and creation of art shows. One of their recent works, featured here, is not really a work of architecture at all, but rather a clever play on surface and meaning in buildings. Their Facsimile installation consists of a large video screen mounted on the façade of the Moscone Center in San Francisco, a building they did not design. The screen is intended to move across the glass surface of the structure, either playing live video feeds from the lobby or prerecorded interior scenes. There is a pertinent artistic and architectural commentary on the building as a setting for a kind of permanent "reality TV show" in this instance that is very much in the spirit of the firm. Diller Scofidio + Renfro are also working in a more usual if still innovative vein on such projects as the refurbishment of Copenhagen's legendary Tivoli Gardens or the new Institute of Contemporary Art in Boston.

## BREAK ON THROUGH (TO THE OTHER SIDE)

A continent away, architects like Thom Mayne, Michael Rotondi, or Eric Owen Moss have been at the cutting edge of California architecture for many years

[1] Horizon Press, New York, 1953

already. They have adapted an approach whose relation to contemporary art—sculpture in particular—seems readily apparent. Rotondi, who founded Morphosis with Thom Mayne in 1976, went on to become a co-founder of SCI-Arc, the influential Southern California Institute of Architecture, whose stated goal is "to produce architects who are truly artists and thus inherently subversive." Moss has again and again renewed his sculptural vocabulary, eviscerating only disused warehouse buildings and other structures in the Culver City area of Los Angeles and using the found pieces of steel or other construction materials to create sculptural extrusions that lend real character and identity to buildings whose only earlier goal had been to provide space.

Although Thom Mayne and Morphosis first came to prominence in the 1980s, Mayne's pivotal role in American architecture was most recently acclaimed by the jury of the 2005 Pritzker Prize, who declared, "Mayne's approach toward architecture and his philosophy is not derived from European modernism, Asian influences, or even from American precedents of the last century. He has sought throughout his career to create an original architecture, one that is truly representative of the unique, somewhat rootless, culture of Southern California, especially the architecturally rich city of Los Angeles. Like the Eameses, Neutra, Schindler, and Gehry before him, Thom Mayne is an authentic addition to the tradition of innovative, exciting architectural talent that flourishes on the West Coast." Lord Palumbo, chairman of the Pritzker jury, said that Mayne's work represents "the seamless fusion of art and technology." In the 1980s, Mayne's work was dubbed "Post-Holocaust" - aloof, austere, downbeat. His 1986 Kate Mantilini Restaurant was described as "Part diagram, part conceptual sketch, part melancholic portrayal of a lost wholeness, artifacts [that] suggest a complex civilization that has been dug up after it has been destroyed by a neutron bomb that has left these skeletons. —A techno-morphic civilization that has lost its way."

## LIVE FROM CHICAGO

The richness of expression and the dialogue with art or sometimes with social issues seen in the work of Morphosis undoubtedly bears some relation, as does other California work, to the presence of Frank O. Gehry. The significance of his contribution was recognized when he received the 1989 Pritzker Prize. In his acceptance speech, he described some of the factors that explain his style: "My artist friends, like Jasper Johns, Bob Rauschenberg, Ed Kienholz and Claes Oldenburg, were working with very inexpensive materials—broken wood and paper—and they were making beauty. These were not superficial details, they were direct, and raised the question in my mind of what beauty was. I chose to use the craft available, and to work with craftsmen and make a virtue out of their limitations. Painting had an immediacy that I craved for in architecture. I explored the process of new construction materials to try giving feeling and spirit to form. In trying to find the essence of my own expression, I fantasized that I was an artist standing before a white canvas deciding what the first move should be."

In a way, with his small residential projects in Santa Monica or Venice, California, Frank O. Gehry had a kind of artistic freedom that sometimes escaped him once he had achieved the fame that the Guggenheim Bilbao and other buildings bought him. His Jay Pritzker Pavilion in Chicago's new Millennium Park (2001–04) might in a sense represent a return to his sources, because it is a singularly artistic work. A sculptural entanglement of billowing stainless-steel ribbons, the Pavilion does serve as an effective concert venue, but it has fewer practical requirements than the Walt Disney Concert Hall in Los Angeles, for example. It is thus freer to approach the state of the work of art that so inspired Gehry's early work. It is a joyous, participative work—one in which art and the general public actually touch each other—a rare feat in the United States or indeed anywhere else.

## FLUFF AND BIRDS

Although Gehry struggled long and hard to be recognized even in Los Angeles, his example may be a more significant one for today's architects than even that of Frank Lloyd Wright, whose ideas and presence are rooted in the 19th century as much as they were in the 20th. In the United States, perhaps even more than in smaller countries, the style of today's architecture is not definable in any ready terms. The calculated white modernism of a Richard Meier coexists with the clever small-scale work of the young New Yorkers Lewis.Tsurumaki.Lewis, for example. LTL was founded in 1993 and has produced such singular projects as the Fluff Bakery, New York (2004). Created at 751 Ninth Avenue in New York for a cost of $250,000, this space has unusual walls and ceilings, created with strips of felt and stained plywood, each individually put in place. Despite their rather sophisticated background, these architects demonstrate with the Fluff Bakery that they are willing to get directly involved in an original, small-scale project. With the Arthouse at the Jones Center featured here and other work in progress, LTL is not likely to remain confined to small spaces for very long. Their innovative, and somewhat iconoclastic, approach has obvious relations to contemporary installation art, for example. Might it be that whereas Wright lectured about an inevitable link between man and nature, today's generation of American architects prefers to wear the many-colored cloak of the artist? A good part of the appeal of contemporary architecture, of a bakery, or a condominium in Manhattan, for example, has to do with being noticed - being different from the competition. Sophisticated technology has in some sense freed the architect from applying rote memory and allowed an explosion of new forms and ideas.

Even relatively large firms, like Boora of Portland, Oregon, have seen the virtue of experimentation and what might be called an artistic method. Such is certainly the case of their 2004 and 2005 work for the TBA Festival. Taking advantage of donations and recycled materials, they created temporary facilities of the Portland Institute of Contemporary Art with radically reduced budgets and a real sense of creativity. In a very different mode, this type of architecture on a shoestring has also been the strong point of the Rural Studio, founded at Auburn University in Alabama by Samuel Mockbee and Dennis K. Ruth in 1993. Rather than an architectural firm in any traditional sense, this is a university program that has encouraged students to create facilities, including housing, a chapel, or a fire station for poor, rural populations. The Birding Tower published in this book is a case in point for a method rather than necessarily being an accomplished work of architecture. One of the students involved in the project, Natalie Butts, responded in an interesting way when asked to estimate the cost of this project, "The reason we do not wish to include the cost," she wrote, "is simply that it is very difficult to estimate the 'real' cost of the tower and boardwalk. There are thousands of undocumented hours of labor and design work done by the students and teacher. And there are hundreds more donated, undocumented hours of geotechnical, engineering, environmental and landscape consulting work." As a result of this approach, no cost figure is cited for the Rural Studio Birding Tower. It is proof, however, of the degree of passion and energy that young students are willing to put into a good cause related to architecture in the United States. Natalie Butts and her colleagues were able to build their "stairway to heaven" and that is a positive statement about the group involved, but also about the spirit of generosity and hard work that formed America. Where money generally rules, there are significant exceptions.

## HAIL TO THE CHIEF

One might intentionally contrast the flimsy tower built by Natalie Butts and her colleagues in Alabama with the much more substantial (and costly) William J. Clinton Presidential Center (Little Rock, Arkansas, 2001–04) designed by Polshek Partnership Architects. Presidential libraries, with the possible exception of I. M. Pei's Kennedy Library, have not been the object of a great deal of architectural invention. Indeed, starting with the example of Washington, D.C., with its massive federal office buildings, there has long been a divorce from what might be called the avant-garde of American architecture and much of its government or public building. With its dynamic elevated form and intelligent relation to the park in which it is located, the Clinton Center breaks the mold and imposes a forward-looking architectural statement that does indeed correspond to the socially and politically responsible actions of the Clinton Administration. The client for this project is not the U.S. Government, but the William J. Clinton Foundation, of course, but the president's significance remains indelibly connected in the public mind to his service in government. Some will joke about Clinton's private life as it influenced his time in office, but the real legacy of the president is better represented here than it was on television or in the press, for example. Other examples of intelligent contemporary architecture in a governmental mode have also been intentionally selected for this book—Richard Meier's elegant San Jose City Hall (San Jose, California, 2002–05) and Antoine Predock's Austin City Hall and Public Plaza (Austin, Texas, 2001–04). Meier remains faithful to his well-proven style, while Predock calls, as is his wont, on the forces of geology and local preoccupations. Creating public architecture with the often limited budgets and large floor areas that it implies is a challenge for any architect. The fact that cities such as San Jose and Austin see fit to call on talented out-of-town architects is a sign that esthetic sensibilities have evolved. Little Rock and Austin are not usually listed as places to see on a typical contemporary-architecture tour, but thanks to James Polshek and Antoine Predock it was possible to create buildings there that are more than functional blocks.

As continued flows of immigrants show, the United States, even in its post-9-11 mode, is still seen as a land of opportunity for many. It is also a place where the suspension of disbelief has allowed Disneyland and Las Vegas to thrive. Money talks, as the time-worn expression goes, and in America it talks louder than in many other countries. And yet, as this book hopefully shows, contemporary architecture is continuing to be inventive and varied in the land of Wright. As Boora or Rural Studio show, sometimes the absence of a budget can be a source of considerable inventiveness. Though it is certainly not always the case: having $192 million to spend, as the City of San Jose did, can also lead to brilliant results when a world-class architect like Richard Meier is given a commission. A new generation represented here by architects such as Asymptote or Lewis.Tsurumaki.Lewis is already stepping in to take up where Frank O. Gehry and others had lead.

Philip Jodidio

# EINLEITUNG

## STAIRWAY TO HEAVEN

»Veränderung ist der einzige unveränderliche Umstand, den man in der Landschaft findet. Doch die Veränderungen sprechen oder singen alle im Einklang mit dem kosmischen Gesetz, das selbst eine edlere Form der Veränderung ist. Diese kosmischen Gesetze sind sowohl die physikalischen Gesetze aller vom Menschen errichteten Strukturen als auch die Gesetze der Landschaft. Der Mensch nimmt immer dann tätig an der Schöpfung teil, wenn er ein Gebäude unter der Sonne auf die Erde stellt. Wenn er überhaupt ein Geburtsrecht besitzt, dann dieses: Er ist nicht weniger ein Zug der Landschaft als die Felsen, Bäume, Bären oder Bienen jener Natur, der er sein Dasein verdankt. Ständig führt ihm die Natur die Wissenschaft ihrer bemerkenswerten Wirtschaftlichkeit der mineralischen und pflanzlichen Strukturen vor, die mit dem unverdorbenen Charakter zusammenstimmen, der sich allenthalben in ihren Formen zeigt.«

FRANK LLOYD WRIGHT, **The Future of Architecture**[1]

Die Worte, die Frank Lloyd Wright gegen Ende seiner langen Laufbahn schrieb, sprechen von Bauwerken, die unvermeidlich mit der Natur verbunden sind. Wrights Auffassung von »organischer« Architektur hatte gewiss in den Vereinigten Staaten und anderswo ihre Gefolgschaft, aber die heutige Lage, eben jene Zukunft, von der Wright sprach, scheint weiter entfernt von den Geboten des größten amerikanischen Architekten des 20. Jahrhunderts, als dieser vielleicht gehofft hatte. Format und Umfang dieses Buches erlauben nicht, einen vollständigen Überblick über die Architektur in den Vereinigten Staaten vorzulegen. Vielmehr wurde eine bestimmte Anzahl neuerer Projekte ausgewählt, ohne dabei einem speziellen Stil den Vorrang zu geben. Die ausgesuchten Projekte und Architekten reichen von den renommierten (Frank O. Gehry) bis zu den weniger bekannten (Michael Jantzen). Dazwischen findet sich eine Vielzahl von Persönlichkeiten, die jede auf ihre Weise die Architekturszene geprägt haben. Einige von ihnen wurden mit dem Pritzker-Preis ausgezeichnet (Gehry, Meier und Thom Mayne von Morphosis), andere sind anerkannte Neuerer wie Eric Owen Moss oder Steven Holl. Sie sind im Osten ansässig (Williams und Tsien, James Stuart Polshek), im Westen (Wes Jones, Boora oder Antoine Predock) und im Süden (Rural Studio). Es gibt Neuerer, die an der Grenze zwischen Virtualität und Realität arbeiten, wie Asymptote und Jantzen, oder aufgehende Sterne wie Diller Scofidio+Renfro und LTL Lewis.Tsurumaki.Lewis. Der Sinn dieser Aufzählung ist es, die Vielfalt dieser Auswahl zu unterstreichen, die als spannende Einführung in eine Welt dienen kann, die anscheinend nicht nur Wright, sondern auch Gropius und Mies hinter sich gelassen hat.

## SEX AND THE CITY

Seit ihrem ersten Auftritt in der Architekturszene mit ihrem 1988 preisgekrönten Auftrag für den Los Angeles West Coast Gateway haben Lise Anne Couture und Hani Rashid von Asymptote die Grenzen der zeitgenössischen Architektur erweitert. Dazu verbinden sie imaginäre Welten, wie bei ihrem Projekt für einen virtuellen Börsensaal in der New York Stock Exchange oder dem virtuellen Gug-

[1] Horizon Press, New York, 1953

genheim Museum, mit realem Bauen. Bei ihrem Carlos Miele Flagship Store an der West 14th Street in Manhattan (2002–03) kombinieren sie ein kühnes Raumgefühl mit einer alles umhüllenden Ausstattung aus hochglänzendem Epoxid und gespanntem PVC-Gummi. Der schon lange an Objekten interessierte Hani Rashid, Bruder des bekannten Designers Karim Rashid, ist dabei, den Sprung zur Gestaltung von Büroobjekten für Alessi zu wagen. Als dieses Buch in den Druck ging, war Asymptote dabei, in New York den neuen Flagship Store von Alessi fertig zu stellen. Hani Rashids Kombination von virtuellen Environments, realer Architektur und Objekten entspricht ganz sicher der derzeitigen Stimmung. Es fällt häufig schwer, Kunst und Architektur vollständig zu trennen, und auch Objekte werden zunehmend in den architektonischen Kontext einbezogen. Diese von technologischen Verbesserungen gestützte Entwicklung baut nicht auf die gleiche Art von utopischem System auf, das die Vorstellung des Bauhauses vom Gesamtkunstwerk inspirierte, aber sie könnte sehr wohl in die gleiche Richtung führen.

Ein künstlerischer Ansatz ist für das Schaffen vieler amerikanischer Architekten kennzeichnend geworden, nicht zuletzt für den in New York ansässigen Steven Holl. Seine Arbeit beginnt ausnahmslos mit aquarellierten Darstellungen, die er akribisch in Alben geordnet in seinem Büro aufbewahrt. Sein hier vorgestelltes Turbulence House entwarf er im Auftrag des Bildhauers Richard Tuttle für einen Ort in New Mexico. Ungeachtet seiner Entstehung aus Steven Holls sensiblen Zeichnungen kam dieses unregelmäßig geformte Wohnhaus durch die Verwendung parametrischen Designs und die Herstellung der ungewöhnlichen Aluminiumhaut zustande. Während man erwartet hätte, Computer dienten hauptsächlich zur Entwicklung mathematisch erzeugter neuer Formen, nutzt Holls Büro sie stattdessen, um die dreidimensionalen Modelle zu kreieren, die er zur Umsetzung eines im Grunde künstlerischen Gedankens benötigt. Die Tatsache, dass vom Turbulence House ein genaues Duplikat in einem Skulpturenpark in Schio bei Vicenza existiert, ist ein weiterer ungewöhnlicher Aspekt.

Holls vor kurzem vollendete Schweizer Residenz in Washington, D. C. (mit Rüssli Architekten) ist ein Fall beispielhafter Zusammenarbeit eines amerikanischen mit einem europäischen Architekturbüro. Die Residenz, gleichzeitig in guter Schweizer Tradition bescheiden und doch weitläufig genug, um zur selben Zeit zweihundert und mehr Gästen Platz zu bieten, erscheint streng und ist doch ausreichend komplex, um Holls charakteristische Licht- und Farbgestaltung zuzulassen. In diesem Fall veranschaulicht Steven Holl, dass die Nachwirkungen der Moderne und ihre Anpassung an heutige Gegebenheiten, integraler Bestandteil der amerikanischen Architektur ist. Seine Bauten sind schöpferisch und doch beständig in Ort und Funktion verankert.

Das ebenfalls in New York beheimatete Büro von Diller Scofidio+Renfro hat sich lange an Entwurf und Gestaltung von Kunstausstellungen beteiligt. Eine ihrer hier gezeigten, neueren Arbeiten ist im Grunde keineswegs ein architektonisches Werk, sondern eher ein Spiel mit Oberfläche und Bedeutung in Bauwerken. Ihre Installation »Facsimile« besteht aus einer großflächigen Videoleinwand, die an der Fassade des nicht von Diller Scofidio+Renfro entworfenen Moscone Centers in San Francisco befestigt ist. Die Leinwand soll sich über die gläserne Oberfläche des

Gebäudes bewegen und dabei das live eingespielte Geschehen aus der Lobby oder vorab aufgezeichnete Innenraumszenen zeigen. Dies bildet einen passenden künstlerischen und architektonischen Kommentar zu dem Gebäude als Schauplatz einer ständigen TV-Realityshow der ausgesprochen gut zum Geist des Büros passt. Diller Scofidio+Renfro arbeiten außerdem in üblicherer, wenngleich ebenfalls innovativer Weise an Projekten wie der Neugestaltung des legendären Tivoliparks in Kopenhagen oder dem neuen Institute of Contemporary Art in Boston.

## BREAK ON THROUGH (TO THE OTHER SIDE)

Auf der anderen Seite des Kontinents gehören Thom Mayne, Michael Rotondi und Eric Owen Moss seit vielen Jahren zur Avantgarde der kalifornischen Architektur. Sie haben eine Vorgehensweise, deren Bezug zur zeitgenössischen Kunst, insbesondere zur Skulptur, augenfällig ist. Rotondi, der gemeinsam mit Thom Mayne 1976 Morphosis begründete, wurde später zum Mitbegründer von SCI-Arc, dem einflussreichen Southern California Institute of Architecture, dessen erklärtes Ziel es ist, »Architekten auszubilden, die wirkliche Künstler und somit subversiv sind«. Moss hat wieder und wieder seine plastische Formensprache erneuert, indem er leer stehende Lagerhäuser und andere Gebäude im Gebiet von Culver City/Los Angeles entkernt und die Fundstücke aus Stahl und anderen Baumaterialien dazu verwendet, skulpturale Objekte zu schaffen. Sie verhelfen Gebäuden, deren früherer Zweck nur darin bestand, Raum zur Verfügung zu stellen, zu Charakter und eigener Identität.

Obwohl Thom Mayne und Morphosis sich schon in den 1980er Jahren hervortaten, wurde Maynes zentrale Rolle in der amerikanischen Architektur erst in jüngster Zeit durch die Jury des Pritzker-Preises 2005 anerkannt, die dazu erklärte: »Maynes Einstellung zur Architektur und seine Philosophie leiten sich nicht von der europäischen Moderne ab, nicht von asiatischen Einflüssen, ja nicht einmal von amerikanischen Vorbildern des letzten Jahrhunderts. Er war während seiner gesamten Laufbahn bestrebt, eine originäre Architektur zu schaffen, eine, die die einzigartige, eher entwurzelte Kultur Südkaliforniens verkörpert, insbesondere jene der mit architektonischem Erbe reich gesegneten Stadt Los Angeles. Wie das Ehepaar Eames, Neutra, Schindler und Gehry vor ihm ist auch Thom Mayne eine echte Bereicherung des traditionell innovativen, anregenden Pools architektonischer Begabungen, der an der Westküste wirkt.« Der Vorsitzende der Pritzker-Jury, Lord Palumbo, sagte, Maynes Œuvre stelle »die nahtlose Verschmelzung von Kunst und Technologie« dar. In den 1980er-Jahren handelte sich Maynes Architektur die Bezeichnung »Post-Holocaust« ein – reserviert, asketisch, unprätentiös. Sein 1986 entstandenes Kate Mantilini Restaurant beschrieb man als »teils konzeptuelle Skizze, teils melancholisches Porträt einer verlorenen Ganzheit, Artefakte [die] auf eine komplexe Zivilisation hindeuten, deren Überreste man nach der Zerstörung durch eine Neutronenbombe ausgegraben hat. – Eine technomorphe Zivilisation, die vom Weg abgekommen ist.«

## LIVE FROM CHICAGO

Die expressive Vielfalt und die im Werk von Morphosis erkennbare Auseinandersetzung mit der Kunst oder bisweilen mit gesellschaftlichen Fragen, steht,

wie auch die Arbeiten anderer, in Zusammenhang mit der Präsenz von Frank O. Gehry. Die Bedeutung seines Beitrags wurde deutlich, als Gehry den Pritzker-Preis 1989 erhielt. In seiner Dankesrede beschrieb er einige der Faktoren, die seinen Stil erklären: »Meine Künstlerfreunde, wie Jasper Johns, Bob Rauschenberg, Ed Kienholz und Claes Oldenburg, arbeiteten mit äußerst kostengünstigen Materialien – Restholz und Papier – und sie erschufen Schönheit. Da handelte es sich nicht um oberflächliche Einzelheiten, sie waren direkt, und mir stellte sich die Frage nach der Definition von Schönheit. Ich entschied mich, das verfügbare Handwerk zu nutzen, mit Handwerkern zu arbeiten und aus ihren Beschränkungen eine Tugend zu machen. Malerei hat eine Unmittelbarkeit, nach der ich mich in der Architektur sehnte. Ich probierte neue Baumaterialien aus in dem Versuch, Formen mit Gefühl und Geist zu erfüllen. Bei dem Versuch, das Wesentliche meines eigenen Ausdrucks zu finden, stellte ich mir vor, ich wäre ein Künstler, der vor einer weißen Leinwand steht und sich über seinen ersten Strich klar werden soll.«

In gewisser Hinsicht hatte Frank O. Gehry bei seinen kleinen Wohnhausprojekten in Santa Monica oder Venice eine künstlerische Freiheit, die ihm zuweilen abhanden kam, seit er durch das Guggenheim Museum in Bilbao und andere Großprojekte zu allgemeiner Bekanntheit gelangte. Sein Jay Pritzker Pavilion in Chicagos neuem Millennium Park (2001–04) stellt in gewisser Weise eine Rückkehr zu seinen Wurzeln dar, weil es sich dabei um ein außerordentlich künstlerisches Werk handelt. Der Pavillon, ein mehr als 36 m hohes, plastisches Gewirr aus schwebenden Edelstahlbändern, dient als eindrucksvoller Ort für Konzerte, muss allerdings weit weniger praktischen Anforderungen genügen als zum Beispiel die komplexe Walt Disney Concert Hall in Los Angeles. Somit kann er sich freier dem Status des Kunstwerks annähern, der Gehrys frühes Schaffen so inspirierte. Es ist ein fröhliches, zur Beteiligung einladendes Werk, eines, in dem sich Kunst und Öffentlichkeit tatsächlich berühren – ein in den Vereinigten Staaten wie auch anderswo seltenes Meisterstück.

## FLUFF AND BIRDS

Obwohl Gehry sogar in Los Angeles lang und hart um Anerkennung kämpfen musste, ist seine Vorbildwirkung für die heutige Architektur vielleicht noch bedeutsamer, als selbst die von Frank Lloyd Wright, dessen Ideen und Präsenz ebenso nachhaltig im 19. wie im 20. Jahrhundert verwurzelt sind. In den Vereinigten Staaten ist der Stil der heutigen Architektur vielleicht noch schwieriger in fertige Begriffe zu fassen als in kleineren Ländern. So existiert die kalkulierte Weiße Moderne eines Richard Meier zum Beispiel neben den kleinteiligen Arbeiten des jungen New Yorker Büros Lewis.Tsurumaki.Lewis. Es wurde 1993 begründet und hat seither solch außerordentliche Projekte wie die Bäckerei Fluff, New York (2004) geschaffen. Dieser mit einem Budget von 250 000 Dollar realisierte, 75 m² große Raum entstand an der Ninth Avenue 751 in New York. Er zeichnet sich durch ungewöhnliche Wände und Decken aus, die mit jeweils einzeln verlegten Streifen von Filz und gebeiztem Sperrholz verkleidet sind. Ungeachtet ihres eher intellektuellen Hintergrunds beweisen LTL mit der Bäckerei Fluff, dass sie willens sind, sich unmittelbar auf ein originelles, kleinformatiges Projekt einzulassen. Angesichts des hier vorgestellten Arthouse im Jones Center und anderer, im Bau befindlicher Projekte erscheint es wenig wahrscheinlich, dass LTL lange auf kleine Räume beschränkt bleiben wird. Ihr innovativer, ein wenig bilderstürmerischer Ansatz weist zum Beispiel augenfällige Beziehungen zu aktuellen künstlerischen Installationen auf. Könnte es sein, dass die heutige Generation amerikanischer Architekten es vorzieht, den bunten Umhang des Künstlers zu tragen, anstatt wie einst Frank Lloyd Wright an die unvermeidliche Verbindung zwischen Mensch und Natur zu glauben? Ein Gutteil der Wirkung zeitgenössischer Architektur, zum Beispiel einer Bäckerei oder einer Eigentumswohnung in Manhattan, besteht darin, dass sie Aufsehen erregt, sich von der Konkurrenz unterscheidet. Hochentwickelte Technologie befreite die Architekten in gewissem Sinn von der Anwendung mechanischer Routine und ermöglichte eine sprunghafte Zunahme neuer Formen und Ideen.

Selbst relativ große Büros wie Boora aus Portland, Oregon, haben die Vorzüge des Experimentierens und der so genannten künstlerischen Vorgehensweise erkannt. In diese Kategorie fallen sicherlich die 2004 und 2005 entstandenen Arbeiten für das TBA Festival. Mit minimalen Budgets, großer Kreativität und indem es Spenden und aufbereitete Materialien nutzte, schuf das Büro Boora temporäre Einrichtungen für das Portland Institute of Contemporary Art. Auf ganz andere Weise ist diese Art von Minimalarchitektur auch die Stärke von Rural Studio, das 1993 von Samuel Mockbee und Dennis K. Ruth an der Auburn University in Alabama gegründet wurde. Es handelt sich hier nicht um ein herkömmliches Architekturbüro, sondern um ein Universitätsprogramm, das Studenten ermuntert, für arme Bevölkerungsgruppen auf dem Land Einrichtungen wie Wohnhäuser, eine Kapelle oder eine Feuerwache zu konzipieren. Der hier gezeigte Turm zur Beobachtung von Vögeln dient als typisches Beispiel für eine Methodik und nicht unbedingt als vollendetes Werk der Architektur. Natalie Butts, eine der an diesem Projekt beteiligten Studentinnen, gab eine interessante Antwort auf die Frage nach den Kosten des Turms. »Der Grund, weshalb wir die Kosten nicht angeben möchten«, schrieb sie, »ist einfach der, dass es sehr schwierig ist, die ›wirklichen‹ Kosten des Turms und des Holzstegs zu beziffern. Es wurden von den Studenten und ihrem Lehrer Tausende nicht erfasster Arbeitsstunden geleistet. Und darüber hinaus wurden wir von Geotechnikern, Bautechnikern, Umweltexperten und Landschaftsgestaltern unterstützt, die Hunderte von freiwillig gestifteten, ebenfalls undokumentierten Stunden zur Verfügung stellten.« Folglich werden für den »Birding Tower« von Rural Studio keine Baukosten angeführt. Das Projekt kann jedoch als Beleg für das Maß an Leidenschaft und Energie dienen, das junge Studenten in einen mit Architektur verknüpften guten Zweck investieren. Natalie Butts und ihre Mitstreiter konnten ihre »Treppe zum Himmel« bauen, und dies ist eine positive Aussage sowohl über die beteiligte Gruppe als auch über den Geist der Großzügigkeit und der harten Arbeit, der Amerika formte. Von der Regel, wonach Geld die Welt beherrscht, gibt es offenbar bemerkenswerte Ausnahmen.

## HAIL TO THE CHIEF

Man könnte bewusst den von Natalie Butts und ihren Mitstreitern in Alabama errichteten, eher provisorisch anmutenden Turm mit dem wesentlich gediegeneren (und kostspieligeren) William J. Clinton Presidential Center, Little Rock, Arkansas (2001–04) vergleichen, das von Polshek Partnership Architects konzipiert wurde. Abgesehen höchstens von Ieoh Ming Peis Kennedy Library zeichnen sich die den Präsidenten zugeeigneten Bibliotheksbauten nicht eben durch übermäßigen architektonischen Einfallsreichtum aus. Angefangen mit Washington D.C. und den wuchtigen Bürobauten der Bundesregierung besteht seit langem ein Bruch zwischen der so genannten Avantgarde der amerikanischen Architektur und einem Großteil der Regierungs- und öffentlichen Gebäude. Mit seiner dynamisch-erhöhten Form und der durchdachten Beziehung zum umgebenden Parkgelände sprengt das Clinton Center den üblichen Rahmen und imponiert mit einer in die Zukunft gerichteten, architektonischen Form, die dem gesellschaftlich und politisch verantwortungsvollen Handeln der Clinton-Regierung entspricht. Der Auftraggeber ist nicht die amerikanische Regierung, sondern natürlich die William J. Clinton Foundation, aber die Bedeutung Clintons bleibt in der öffentlichen Meinung unauslöschlich mit seiner Präsidententätigkeit verbunden. Man mag sich darüber amüsieren, wie Clintons Privatleben seine Amtszeit beeinflusst hat, aber das wahre Vermächtnis des Präsidenten ist besser hier repräsentiert als zum Beispiel im Fernsehen oder in der Presse. Andere Beispiele für kluge zeitgenössische Architektur im Auftrag der Regierung wurden ebenso bewusst für dieses Buch ausgewählt - Richard Meiers elegante City Hall in San Jose, Kalifornien (2002–05) sowie Antoine Predocks City Hall und Public Plaza für Austin, Texas (2001–04). Meier bleibt seinem erprobten Stil treu, während sich Predock wie gewohnt auf die Kräfte der Geologie und lokale Vorlieben beruft. Die Gestaltung öffentlicher Bauten mit ihren meist knappen Budgets und großen Geschossflächen bedeutet für jeden Architekten eine Herausforderung. Der Umstand, dass Städte wie San Jose und Austin es für richtig halten, begabte, auswärtige Architekten heranzuziehen, ist ein Zeichen für zunehmendes ästhetisches Verständnis. Little Rock und Austin stehen üblicherweise nicht auf der Liste jener Orte, die man auf einer Tour zur Besichtigung zeitgenössischer Architektur aufsucht, gleichwohl war es dank James Polshek und Antoine Predock möglich, dort Bauten zu errichten, die über die reine Funktionalität hinausgehen.

Wie der anhaltende Zustrom von Einwanderern zeigt, werden die Vereinigten Staaten selbst nach dem 9. September 2001 von vielen Menschen als ein chancenreiches Land angesehen. Außerdem sind sie ein Ort, an dem die zeitweilige Aufhebung des Zweifelns Disneyland und Las Vegas florieren lässt. Geld regiert die Welt - wie das abgedroschene Sprichwort sagt - und in Amerika scheint das stärker als in manch anderen Ländern so zu sein. Wie dieses Buch hoffentlich zeigen kann, bleibt die zeitgenössische Architektur im Lande Wrights trotzdem innovativ und vielfältig. Wie Boora oder Rural Studio demonstrieren, kann ein knappes Budget bisweilen beachtlichen Einfallsreichtum freisetzen. Ebenso kann die Gelegenheit, 192 Millionen Dollar auszugeben, wie im Fall von San Jose, zu hervorragenden Ergebnissen führen, wenn ein Architekt von Weltklasse wie Richard Meier den Auftrag erhält. Eine neue Generation von Architekten wie Asymptote oder Lewis.Tsurumaki.Lewis steht bereit, da weiterzumachen, wo Frank O. Gehry und andere aufhörten.

Philip Jodidio

# INTRODUCTION

## UN ESCALIER POUR LE PARADIS

« Le changement est la seule constante immuable dans le paysage. Mais tous les changements parlent de la loi cosmique ou la chantent à l'unisson, elle qui est une forme noble du changement. Les lois cosmiques sont les lois physiques s'appliquant à toute structure construite par l'homme ainsi qu'au paysage. L'homme participe positivement à la création lorsqu'il élève une construction sur la terre et sous le soleil. S'il existe un droit qu'il possède de naissance, ce doit bien être celui-ci : lui aussi n'est pas moins un élément du paysage que les rochers, les arbres, les ours ou les abeilles, ou que la nature à laquelle il doit son être. La nature lui montre en permanence la science de sa remarquable économie de structure dans les constructions minérales et végétales qui accompagnent le caractère préservé qui apparaît dans toutes ses formes ».

FRANK LLOYD WRIGHT, **The Future of Architecture**[1]

Ce texte que Frank Lloyd Wright écrivit vers la fin de sa longue carrière nous parle de constructions inéluctablement liées à la nature. La conception wrightienne de l'architecture « organique » a certainement eu des adeptes aux États-Unis et ailleurs, mais la situation actuelle, le futur même dont il parlait, semblent plus distants des préceptes du plus grand des architectes américains du XXe siècle qu'il ne l'aurait espéré. La forme et les dimensions de ce livre ne permettent pas d'offrir un survol complet de l'architecture américaine, mais plutôt une sélection de réalisations récentes, sans vouloir défendre quelque style que ce soit. Les projets et les architectes retenus vont d'acteurs très célèbres, comme Frank O. Gehry, à d'autres encore peu connus, comme Michael Jantzen, en passant par toute une diversité d'intervenants qui ont, chacun à sa façon, marqué la scène architecturale. On trouve des Pritzker Prize (Gehry, Meier, Thom Mayne) mais aussi des novateurs reconnus (Eric Owen Moss, Steven Holl). Ils peuvent travailler sur la côte Est (William & Tsien, James Stuart Polshek), ou la côte Ouest (Wes Jones, Boora, Antoine Predock) ou dans le Sud (Rural Studio). Certains opèrent à la frontière entre le réel et le virtuel comme Asymptote et Jantzen, d'autres sont des stars montantes comme Diller Scofidio + Renfro ou LTL Lewis.Tsurumaki.Lewis. Cette énumération a pour simple objectif de montrer la variété de cette sélection qui se propose d'abord d'offrir une introduction motivante à un monde qui semble avoir laissé loin derrière lui non seulement Wright mais aussi Gropius et Mies.

## SEX AND THE CITY

Depuis leur première apparition sur la scène architecturale qui les vit remporter le concours de la Los Angeles West Coast Gateway, Lise Anne Couture et Hahni Rashid d'Asymptote semblent vouloir repousser les limites de l'architecture contemporaine par des environnements imaginaires, comme dans leurs propositions pour une salle de marché de la bourse de New York ou le Guggenheim Virtual Museum, mais aussi la réalisation de projets concrets. Le magasin vaisseau amiral de Carlos Miele sur West 14th Street à Manhattan (2002-03) associe un sens aigu de l'espace et un enveloppement en époxy hyper brillant ou caoutchouc PVC

étiré. S'intéressant depuis longtemps aux objets, Hani Rashid, frère du célèbre designer Karim Rashid, s'est plongé dans la création active de produits pour le bureau pour Alessi. Asymptote vient juste de terminer le magasin modèle d'Alessi à New York au moment de la mise sous presse de ce livre. Cette combinaison d'environnements virtuels, d'architecture concrète et d'objets est parfaitement dans l'air du temps. Il est souvent difficile de séparer complètement l'art et l'architecture, et le design s'oriente vers une intégration toujours plus grande à l'environnement architectural. Ce mouvement soutenu par divers progrès technologiques ne puise pas aux sources du même contexte intellectuel que l'idée de Gesamtkunstwerk du Bauhaus mais pourrait bien s'orienter dans la même direction que ce qui avait été imaginé à cette époque en Allemagne.

L'approche artistique est en fait devenue la marque des travaux de nombreux architectes américains, parmi lesquels Steven Holl, basé à New York, n'est pas des moindres. Son processus de conception débute systématiquement par des études à l'aquarelle, méticuleusement classées dans des albums qu'il conserve dans son agence. Son projet publié ici, la Turbulence House, a été conçue pour le sculpteur Richard Tuttle sur un terrain au Nouveau-Mexique. Même si elle est d'abord apparue sous la forme des dessins empreints de sensibilité de Steven Holl, cette résidence de forme irrégulière dessinée à l'aide d'un logiciel de conception paramétrique est habillée d'une surprenante peau d'aluminium. Alors que les ordinateurs sont souvent et surtout utilisés pour mettre au point des formes mathématiquement viables, l'agence Holl s'en sert plutôt pour créer les maquettes en trois dimensions nécessaires à la réalisation d'un projet de nature fondamentalement artistique. Un autre aspect curieux de cette maison est qu'elle possède sa jumelle, édifiée dans un parc de sculptures à Schio, près de Vicence en Italie.

La résidence de l'ambassadeur de Suisse à Washington récemment achevée est un exemple de collaboration exemplaire entre une agence américaine (Holl) et une agence suisse (Rüssli Architects). Sous des dehors austères imputables à la sobriété de sa conception dans la bonne tradition suisse, cette résidence est suffisament vaste pour accueillir plus de deux cents invités à la fois et suffisament complexe pour permettre à Steven Holl de se livrer à ses subtils jeux de lumière et sur les couleurs. Ici, l'architecte montre que l'influence du mouvement moderne et son adaptation au contexte d'aujourd'hui font partie intégrante de l'architecture américaine. Son œuvre est à la fois originale et néanmoins fermement enracinée dans le site et respectueuse de la fonction.

Une autre agence new-yorkaise, Diller Scofidio + Renfro participe depuis longtemps à la conception d'expositions d'art. L'une de leurs récentes interventions, présentée ici, n'est pas vraiment une œuvre d'architecture mais plutôt un jeu intelligent sur les notions de surface et de sens dans le bâti. Leur installation Facsimile consiste en un grand écran vidéo monté sur la façade du Moscone Center à San Francisco, bâtiment qu'ils n'ont pas construit. L'écran doit se déplacer sur la surface de verre de la façade tout en diffusant des images prises en direct dans le hall d'accueil ou des scènes préenregistrées prises de l'intérieur. Il s'agit donc d'un commentaire artistique et architectural pertinent sur l'immeuble en tant que cadre

---

[1] Horizon Press, New York, 1953

d'un reality-show télévisuel permanent tout à fait dans l'esprit de cette agence. Diller Scofidio + Renfro travaillent également dans une veine plus fonctionnelle mais tout aussi novatrice sur des projets comme la réhabilitation du légendaire parc d'attraction de Copenhague, Tivoli, ou le nouvel Institute of Contemporary Art à Boston.

## DE L'AUTRE CÔTÉ

De l'autre côté du continent, des architectes comme Thom Mayne, Michael Rotondi ou Eric Owen Moss campent depuis de nombreuses années déjà à l'avant-garde de l'architecture californienne. Ils ont développé une approche dont la relation avec l'art contemporain, – la sculpture en particulier – est manifeste. Rotondi, fondateur de Morphosis avec Thom Mayne en 1976, a poursuivi seul son chemin et a cofondé SCI-Arc, l'influent Southern California Institute of Architecture, dont le but affiché est « de produire des architectes qui sont des artistes authentiques et donc nécessairement subversifs. » Moss a sans cesse renouvelé son vocabulaire sculptural dans ses éviscérations d'entrepôts abandonnés et autres constructions du quartier de Culver City à Los Angeles, et dans son utilisation de pièces d'acier et de matériaux de récupération pour créer des extrusions sculpturales qui donnent un caractère et une identité propre à des bâtiments dont la fonction d'origine n'était que d'offrir de l'espace.

Bien que Thom Mayne et Morphosis soient apparus sur la scène architecturale dans les années 1980, ce n'est que très récemment que le rôle fondamental de Mayne dans l'architecture américaine a été consacré par l'attribution du Pritzker Prize 2005. Le jury a déclaré : « L'approche de l'architecture de Mayne et sa philosophie ne proviennent pas du modernisme européen, ni d'influences asiatiques ni même de précédents américains du siècle dernier. Il a cherché tout au long de sa carrière à créer une architecture originale, authentiquement représentative de la culture unique et d'une certaine façon sans racine du Sud de la Californie, en particulier de la ville de Los Angeles connue pour la richesse de son architecture. Comme les Eames, Neutra, Schindler et Gehry avant lui, Thom Mayne représente une authentique contribution à la tradition de talents architecturaux novateurs et fascinants qui se développe sur la Côte Ouest. » Lord Palumbo, président du jury, a par ailleurs précisé que l'œuvre de Mayne représente « une fusion d'art et de technologie sans rupture apparente. » Dans les années 1980, le travail de Mayne avait été affublé du qualificatif de style « post-holocauste » abstrait, austère et déprimant. Son Kate Mantilini Restaurant était jugé « en partie un plan, en partie un croquis de concept, en partie le portrait mélancolique d'une globalité perdue, un artefact [qui] suggère une civilisation complexe mise au jour après avoir été détruite par une bombe aux neutrons qui n'aurait laissé que ces squelettes... une civilisation technomorphique qui aurait perdu son orientation. »

## EN DIRECT DE CHICAGO

La richesse d'expression, le dialogue avec l'art et parfois la prise en compte des enjeux sociaux que l'on constate dans le travail de Morphosis portent sans aucun doute la marque - comme chez d'autres Californiens — de la forte présence de Frank O. Gehry. Le poids de sa contribution a été salué par l'attribution du Pritzker Prize 1989. Dans son discours d'acceptation, Gehry a expliqué certains éléments qui éclairent son style : « Mes amis artistes, comme Jasper Johns, Bob Rauschenberg, Ed Kienholz et Claes Oldenburg travaillaient avec des matériaux très bon marché – morceaux de bois, papier – et donnaient naissance à de la beauté. Il ne s'agissait pas de détails superficiels, mais d'une expression directe qui soulevait chez moi la question de la beauté. J'ai choisi d'utiliser le savoir-faire disponible, de travailler avec des artisans et de faire de leurs limites une vertu. La peinture offrait l'immédiateté dont je rêvais pour l'architecture. J'ai exploré le processus de mise en œuvre de nouveaux matériaux de construction pour essayer de donner à la forme un sentiment et un esprit. En essayant de trouver l'essence de ma propre expression, je me suis pris à imaginer que j'étais un artiste devant une toile blanche décidant du premier geste qu'il allait faire. »

On peut remarquer que dans ses petits projets de maisons pour Santa Monica ou Venice, Frank O. Gehry bénéficiait d'une liberté artistique qui lui a échappé, après qu'il a accédé à la notoriété grâce au Guggenheim de Bilbao et d'autres réalisations. Son Jay Pritzker Pavilion dans le New Millenium Park de Chicago (2001-04) pourrait en un sens représenter un retour à ses sources, tellement il est singulier. Se présentant sous forme d'un enchevêtrement de 36 m de haut de rubans d'acier inoxydable, ce pavillon soumis à moins de contraintes pratiques que le complexe du Walt Disney Concert Hall à Los Angeles est une salle de concert qui fonctionne parfaitement. Gehry a ainsi été plus libre d'approcher l'état d'œuvre d'art qui avait inspiré ses travaux antérieurs. C'est une œuvre joyeuse qui incite à la participation – l'art et le grand public peuvent échanger – un festin architectural rare aussi bien aux États-unis qu'ailleurs.

## FLUFF AND BIRDS (DES GÂTEAUX AUX OISEAUX)

Bien que Gehry se soit durement et longuement battu avant d'être reconnu, même à Los Angeles, son exemple est peut-être plus signifiant pour les architectes d'aujourd'hui que celui de Frank Lloyd Wright, dont les idées et l'apport sont autant enracinés dans le XIXe que le XXe siècle. Aux États-Unis, peut-être plus encore que dans des pays moins grands, le style de l'architecture actuelle ne peut se redéfinir en termes pré-formatés. Le modernisme « blanc » et intensément calculé de Richard Meier peut coexister avec les réalisations intelligentes à petite échelle des jeunes new Yorkais Lewis.Tsurumaki.Lewis. L'agence LTL, fondée en 1993, est à l'origine de projets aussi singuliers que la Fluff Bakery, New York (2004). Situé au 751 9th Avenue et aménagé pour un budget de 250 000 dollars, cet espace de 75 m² présente de curieux murs et plafonds recouverts de bandeaux de feutre et de contreplaqué teinté, mis en place un par un. Malgré leur formation assez sophistiquée, ces architectes ont prouvé ici qu'ils n'hésitent pas à s'impliquer directement dans un projet original même à petite échelle. Avec l'Arthouse du Jones Center publiée ici et d'autres chantiers en cours, l'agence LTL ne restera sans doute pas confinée longtemps dans ces petits espaces. Son approche novatrice et quelque peu iconoclaste entretient des relations évidentes avec l'art d'installation, par exemple. À l'enseignement de Wright sur le lien incontournable entre l'homme et la nature, la nouvelle génération des architectes américains préfèrerait-elle l'approche de l'artiste ? L'architecture contemporaine, qu'elle se manifeste dans une boulangerie ou dans un immeuble d'habitation à Manhattan, semble en général vouloir créer un effet de surprise et afficher sa différence. En un sens, la sophistication des technologies a libéré l'architecte de l'application de recettes mécaniques et a permis une explosion de formes et d'idées nouvelles.

Même des agences relativement importantes comme Boora de Portland (Oregon) ont reconnu les vertus de l'expérimentation et de ce que l'on pourrait appeler la méthode artistique. C'est certainement le cas de leurs interventions en 2004 et 2005 pour le TBA Festival. Grâce à des dons de matériaux recyclés, ils ont créé des installations temporaires pour le Portland Institute of Contemporary Art avec des budgets extrêmement serrés non sans une brillante créativité. Dans un mode très différent, ce type d'architecture à peu de frais est également le point fort de Rural Studio, fondé à Auburn University en Alabama par Samuel Mockbee et Dennis K. Ruth en 1993. Plutôt que d'une agence au sens traditionnel, il s'agit d'un programme universitaire qui encourage les étudiants à créer des installations pour des populations rurales pauvres tels que des logements, une chapelle ou une caserne de pompiers. La Birding Tower (Tour aux oiseaux) publiée ici est un exemple d'une méthode plutôt qu'une œuvre d'architecture accomplie. L'une des étudiantes participant à ce projet, Natalie Butts, a apporté une réponse intéressante lorsqu'elle a été interrogée sur le coût de ce projet : « La raison pour laquelle nous ne souhaitons pas parler de coût, est simplement qu'il est très difficile d'estimer le coût "réel" de la tour et de l'allée de planches. On n'a pas tenu de registre des milliers d'heures de travail et de conception effectuées par les étudiants et le professeur. Ni des centaines d'heures supplémentaires d'ingénierie, de géotechnique, de travail de consultance pour l'environnement et le paysage. » En fait, aucun coût n'est cité pour cette tour. Elle illustre cependant une preuve du degré de passion et d'énergie que de jeunes étudiants sont prêts à insuffler dans une bonne cause en relation avec l'architecture. Natalie Butts et ses condisciples ont pu construire leur « escalier vers le paradis » dans une attitude positive de groupe qui correspond aussi à l'esprit de générosité et de dur labeur qui est à l'origine des États-Unis. L'argent ne règne pas toujours en maître absolu.

## HOMMAGE AU PRÉSIDENT

On pourrait s'amuser à opposer la tour de Rural Studio en Alabama avec le William J. Clinton Presidential Center (Little Rock, Arkansas, 2001–04), projet beaucoup plus vaste – et coûteux – conçu par Polshek Partnership Architects. Les bibliothèques présidentielles, à l'exception éventuellement de la Kennedy Library de I. M. Pei, ne font généralement pas preuve d'une grande inventivité architecturale. Si l'on part de l'exemple de la capitale fédérale et de ses massifs bâtiments officiels, il est certain qu'un divorce a longtemps existé entre l'avant-garde de l'architecture américaine et une grande partie de ses bâtiments publics. Par sa forme dynamique en suspension et sa relation intelligente avec le parc dans lequel il est situé, le Clinton Center casse le moule et impose une approche architecturale prospective qui correspond d'ailleurs au programme social et politique de l'administration de ce président. Le client ici n'était pas le gouvernement mais la William J. Clinton Foundation, et le projet reste indélébilement associé dans l'esprit du public aux mandats de

l'élu. Certains plaisanteront sur sa vie privée qui a pu influencer son passage aux affaires, mais son apport est mieux présenté ici qu'il ne l'était à la télévision ou dans la presse. D'autres exemples d'architecture contemporaine publique intelligente ont été volontairement sélectionnés pour ce livre, comme l'élégant Civic Center de San Jose par Richard Meier (San Jose, Californie 2002–05) et l'Hôtel de ville et sa plazza à Austin par Antoine Predock (Austin, Texas, 2001–04). Meier reste fidèle à son style éprouvé tandis que Predock s'appuie sur les forces tectoniques et les préoccupations locales. Créer une architecture de service public pour des budgets souvent limités et des surfaces de grandes dimensions est un défi pour tout architecte. Le fait que des villes comme San Jose et Austin aient envie de faire appel à des architectes de talent venus d'ailleurs est un signe que la sensibilité esthétique évolue. Little Rock et Austin ne font généralement pas partie des circuits de l'architecture contemporaine, mais grâce à James Polshek et Antoine Predock il a été possible d'y créer des bâtiments qui sont beaucoup plus que de simples boîtes fonctionnelles.

Comme le montre l'afflux continu d'immigrants, et ce malgré les attentats du 11 septembre 2001, (les États-Unis sont encore considérés par beaucoup comme un pays d'opportunités.) C'est aussi un lieu où le rejet de l'incrédulité et l'optimisme ont permis à Disneyland ou à Las Vegas de se développer. L'argent s'exprime toujours, et aux États-Unis, il s'exprime avec encore plus de force que dans de nombreux autres pays. Et cependant, comme ce livre, espérons-le, le montre, l'architecture contemporaine du pays de Frank Lloyd Wright reste inventive et variée. Comme l'illustrent Boora et Rural Studio, même le manque d'argent peut être la source d'une inventivité considérable. Cependant, si ce n'est pas toujours le cas, pouvoir disposer de 192 millions de dollars comme la ville de San Jose peut conduire à des brillants résultats lorsque la commande est passée à un architecte de classe internationale à l'image de Richard Meier. Une nouvelle génération représentée par des architectes comme Asymptote ou Lewis.Tsurumaki.Lewis est en train de prendre le relais, là où Frank O. Gehry et quelques autres s'étaient arrêtés.

Philip Jodidio

# 1

# ASYMPTOTE

**ASYMPTOTE ARCHITECTURE**
160 Varick Street, 10th floor
New York, New York 10013

Tel: +1 212 343 7333
Fax: +1 212 343 7099
e-mail: info@asymptote.net
Web: www.asymptote.net

**LISE ANNE COUTURE** was born in Montreal in 1959. She received her Bachelor of Architecture degree from Carleton University, Ontario, Canada, and her Master of Architecture degree from Yale in 1986. She has been a Design Critic in the Master of Architecture program at Parsons School of Design, New York. Couture has taught at Yale School of Architecture, Princeton, Harvard, Southern California Institute of Architecture (SCI-Arc) and Columbia. **HANI RASHID** was born in 1958 in Cairo, Egypt. He received his Master of Architecture degree from the Cranbrook Academy of Art, Bloomfield Hills, Michigan, in 1985. He has been Professor of Architecture at Columbia since 1989, and he teaches at the Swiss Federal Institute of Technology (ETH) in Zurich. Together, they created Asymptote in 1988. Projects include their 1988 prize-winning commission for the Los Angeles West Coast Gateway; a commissioned housing project for Brig, Switzerland; and their participation in the 1993 competition for an Art Center in Tours, France (1993). Other work by Asymptote includes a theater festival structure built in Denmark in 1997, a virtual trading floor for the New York Stock Exchange (1998), and the Guggenheim Virtual Museum, a multimedia project aimed at creating an online museum (2000). More recently, Asymptote completed the construction of HydraPier in Harlemmermeer, The Netherlands, a public building housing technology and art located near Schiphol Airport, Amsterdam (2002); the Carlos Miele Flagship Store on West 14th Street in Manhattan, New York (2003); a masterplan for Penang, Malaysia (2005); and a new line of office furniture for Knoll International. They were involved in the design of the 2004 Venice Biennale of Architecture, Metamorph. Current projects include a Crematorium and Memorial Chapel in Rotterdam and a condominium building on Perry Street in New York, featured here. Asymptote's works have been exhibited in numerous European and American museums. In 2004, the office received the Frederick Kiesler Award for their contribution in the fields of art and architecture.

# ALESSI
# FLAGSHIP STORE
# NEW YORK, NY
# 2006

FLOOR AREA: 255 m² (2750 ft.²)
CLIENT: Alessi US Shops
COST: not disclosed

The list of architects and designers who have worked with the Italian firm Alessi reads like a Who's Who of the professions: Aldo Rossi, Michael Graves, and more recently Massimilano Fuksas, Wiel Arets, Greg Lynn, Toyo Ito. The style of Alessi as expressed in its shops has largely been conceived by Alessandro Mendini working in close collaboration with Alberto Alessi. That Alessi asked Hani Rashid to come up not only with a new generic shop design, but also to create a certain number of office objects, is a measure of the importance of this commission. Alessi's flagship store is located at 130 Greene Street in the SoHo area of Manhattan. As the architects explain, "Asymptote's approach to the store, product and brand design developed from a search for new languages predicated on mathematically inspired and derived elegance. In a radical shift away from the post modern staples of historic pastiche, motif, vivid coloration, iconographic and symbolic form, and the like, Asymptote forged an approach taking its cues from fluid and dynamic movement intrinsic in new methods and means in form making today inspired and instigated by digital tools and means, privileging a tectonic play of sophisticated geometric solutions in place of symbolic gestures." What they call a "strategic shift in the aesthetic and formal approach," is clearly the goal of Alessi, intent on changing with the times.

Die Aufzählung derjenigen, die für die italienische Firma Alessi tätig waren, liest sich wie das »Who is Who« der Architekten und Designer: Aldo Rossi, Michael Graves und in jüngerer Zeit Massimiliano Fuksas, Wiel Arets, Greg Lynn und Toyo Ito. In erster Linie ist jedoch der Stil, der in den Alessi Shops zum Ausdruck kommt, das Werk von Alessandro Mendini, der eng mit Alberto Alessi zusammenarbeitet. An der Tatsache, dass Alessi Hani Rashid bat, nicht nur eine neue Gestaltung der Läden zu entwickeln, sondern auch eine bestimmte Anzahl von Büroobjekten zu entwerfen, lässt sich die Bedeutung dieses Auftrags ermessen. Der neue Flagship Store von Alessi befindet sich in der Greene Street 130 im SoHo-Viertel von Manhattan. Die Architekten erläutern ihre Vorgehensweise folgendermaßen: »Asymptotes Ansatz bei der Gestaltung von Laden, Produkt und Markenzeichen ergab sich aus der Suche nach neuen Formensprachen, die auf einer mathematisch inspirierten Eleganz basieren. In radikaler Abkehr von der bevorzugten, postmodernen Zusammenstellung historischer Nachahmungen, Motive, lebhafter Farbigkeit, ikonografischer und symbolischer Formgebung usw. konzipierte Asymptote ein Verfahren, das seinen Ansatz aus der fließenden, dynamischen Bewegung bezieht; diese wiederum ist typisch für heutige Methoden und Wege der Formgebung, die angeregt von digitalen Hilfsprogrammen anstelle symbolischer Gesten das tektonische Spiel komplizierter, geometrischer Lösungen bevorzugt.« Das, was sie eine »strategische Verschiebung des ästhetischen und formalen Ansatzes« nennen, deckt sich eindeutig mit dem von Alessi angestrebten Ziel des Wandels im Einklang mit den Zeitläuften.

Aldo Rossi, Michael Graves et plus récemment, Massimiliano Fuksas, Wiel Arets, Greg Lynn et Toyo Ito : la liste des architectes et designers qui ont travaillé pour la firme italienne Alessi est un peu le Who's Who de ces professions. Mais le style qu'exprime ses magasins est l'ouvrage d'Alessandro Mendini en collaboration étroite avec Alberto Alessi. Que l'entreprise ait demandé à Hani Rashid de travailler non seulement sur un nouveau modèle de magasin mais aussi de créer un certain nombre d'objets pour le bureau donne une mesure de l'importance de cette commande. Le nouveau « vaisseau amiral » d'Alessi est situé 130 Green Street dans le quartier de Soho, à Manhattan. Comme l'expliquent les architectes : « L'approche Asymptote de ce magasin, des produits et de l'image de marque a été mise au point à partir d'une recherche de nouveaux langages visant une élégance d'inspiration mathématique. S'éloignant radicalement des tentatives postmodernes de pastiche historique, de motifs, de couleurs vives, de formes iconographiques et symboliques etc., Asymptote s'est forgé son approche en s'appuyant sur le mouvement fluide et dynamique intrinsèque aux nouvelles méthodes et moyens d'élaboration de forme d'aujourd'hui inspirés et facilités par des outils et moyens numériques, et en privilégiant un jeu tectonique de solutions géométriques sophistiquées en lieu et place de gestes symboliques. » Ce qu'Asymptote appelle « une évolution stratégique dans l'approche formelle et esthétique » est clairement devenu l'objectif d'Alessi, qui veut être en phase avec son temps.

# 166 PERRY STREET
# NEW YORK, NY
# 2007

FLOOR AREA: 4645 m² (50 000 ft.²)
CLIENT: Perry Street Development Corporation
COST: not disclosed

With this project, which the architects have called "Surfaced Space," Asymptote enters the very active market in Manhattan for condominium buildings designed by famous architects. Richard Meier has carried the most talked-about intervention of this nature forward with three 16-story apartment towers on Charles Street, next to the site that Hani Rashid and Lise Anne Couture are working on. Situated at the extreme west of Greenwich Village, near the Hudson, the area offers a mix of traditional low-rise buildings and residences and the strong presence of Meier's modernism. As Hani Rashid explains, his design "is in many ways simultaneously antidotal as it is a formal and tectonic playing off of the Meier projects." More specifically, he continues, "Asymptote's approach primarily emerged from a search for an apropos musical assembly of glass and geometry whereby a play of reflections, atmosphere and surface produce an envelope of effects that would weld the disparities of brick, ornament and stoops with glass, smoothness and constant plays of surface and space, resulting in another definition of elegance possibly transcending that of the high modernist traditions and minimalist aspirations expressed in the adjacent towers and the quaintness and scale of domesticity that the building is situated in."

Mit diesem, von den Architekten »Surfaced Space« genannten Projekt betritt Asymptote den in Manhattan bestens florierenden Markt für Eigentumswohnanlagen berühmter Architekten. Richard Meier setzte das meistbesprochene Projekt dieser Art mit drei 16-stöckigen Wohntürmen an der Charles Street um, neben dem Gelände, auf dem gegenwärtig Hani Rashid und Lise Anne Couture tätig sind. Dieses im äußersten Westen von Greenwich Village nahe dem Hudson gelegene Gebiet zeichnet sich durch eine Mischung aus traditionellen, niedrigen Gebäuden und Wohnhäusern sowie der prägenden Präsenz von Meiers Modernismus aus. Wie Hani Rashid erläutert, ist sein Entwurf »in vieler Hinsicht zugleich ein Gegenmittel und eine formale und tektonische Auseinandersetzung mit den Meier'schen Bauten«. Und er fährt fort: »Asymptotes Ansatz ergab sich in erster Linie aus der Suche nach einer gleichsam musikalischen Kombination von Glas und Geometrie, in der das Spiel von Reflexionen, Atmosphäre und Oberfläche eine Hülle von Emotionen entstehen lässt, in der die Unterschiede von Backstein, Ornament und Eingangsterrassen mit Glas, Glätte und dem beständigen Spiel von Oberfläche und Raum verschmelzen. So könnte eine andere Definition von Eleganz entstehen, die möglicherweise hinausgeht über die Traditionen der Hochmoderne und die minimalistischen Ambitionen der benachbarten Türme sowie die malerische Eigenart und das Ausmaß der Häuslichkeit, von denen das Gebäude umgeben ist.«

À travers ce projet baptisé « Surfaced Space » (espace surfacé), Asymptote prend pied sur le marché, très actif à Manhattan, des immeubles d'appartements en copropriété conçus par des architectes célèbres. Richard Meier a réalisé le projet le plus remarqué de ce secteur, une tour de 16 niveaux sur Charles Street, non loin du terrain sur lequel travaillent Hani Rashid et Lise Anne Couture. Situé à l'extrémité ouest de Greenwich Village près de l'Hudson, ce quartier associe librement maisons et petits immeubles à la forte présence du modernisme meierien. Comme l'explique Hani Rashid, son projet « est à de nombreux égards à la fois un antidote et un jeu formel et tectonique par rapport aux projets de Meier. » Plus spécifiquement, « l'approche d'Asymptote est essentiellement venue d'une recherche autour d'un assemblage rythmé de verre et de géométrie dans lequel un jeu de reflets, d'atmosphère et de surfaces produit une enveloppe d'affects qui devrait souder les disparités de la brique, de l'ornement et des piliers par le caractère lisse du verre et les jeux constants des surfaces et des volumes. Il en résulte en une définition autre de l'élégance, qui transcende d'une certaine façon celle des traditions modernistes et des aspirations minimalistes exprimées dans les tours voisines mais aussi le pittoresque et l'échelle domestique des immeubles environnants. »

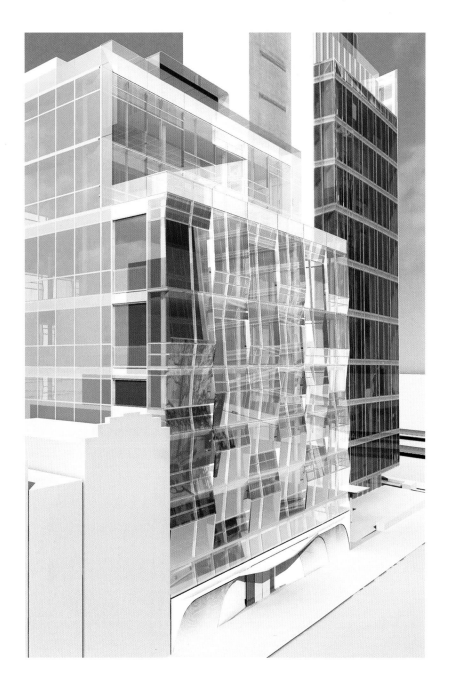

The quiet residential neighborhood near Perry Street and Charles Street has been transformed, initially through the arrival of apartment buildings designed by Richard Meier and, now, with Asymptote's project. The flowing lines typical of their designs are most visible near the entrance.

Die ruhige Wohngegend um Perry Street und Charles Street erfuhr ihre erste Umgestaltung durch die Errichtung von Wohnbauten nach Richard Meiers Entwürfen und nun eine weitere durch das Projekt von Asymptote. Die für die Entwürfe dieses Büros typischen fließenden Linien sind im Eingangsbereich am augenfälligsten.

Le tranquille quartier résidentiel de Perry Street et de Charles Street a été transformé par l'arrivée des immeubles d'habitation de Richard Meier puis par le projet d'Asymptote. Les lignes fluides caractéristiques de leurs interventions sont apparentes en particular près de l'entrée.

The lower floors of the building stand out from the main block and give both a certain transparency and a feeling of movement to the structure, which is located very close to the Hudson River. Perry Street runs perpendicular to the West Side Highway and is close to West 10th Street.

Die unteren Geschosse nahe des Hudson River liegenden Gebäudes springen vor den Hauptbaukörper vor, was dem Bau eine gewisse Transparenz und den Eindruck von Bewegung verleiht. Perry Street verläuft rechtwinklig zum West Side Highway und befindet sich in der Nähe der West 10th Street.

Les niveaux inférieurs sont détachés du bloc principal, conférant à la fois une certaine transparence et une impression de mouvement à cette structure située à proximité immédiate de l'Hudson River. Perry Street est perpendiculaire à la West Side Highway, proche de West 10th Street.

# 2

# BOHLIN CYWINSKI JACKSON

**BOHLIN CYWINSKI JACKSON**
8 West Market Street, Suite 1200
Wilkes-Barre, Pennsylvania 18701

Tel: +1 570 825 8756
Fax: +1 570 825 3744
e-mail: info@bcj.com
Web: www.bcj.com

Bohlin Cywinski Jackson was founded in 1965 by Peter Bohlin and Richard Powell in Wilkes-Barre, Pennsylvania. **PETER BOHLIN** received a Bachelor of Architecture degree from Rensselaer Polytechnic Institute (1959), and a Master of Architecture degree from the Cranbrook Academy of Art (1961). Today the principals are Peter Bohlin, **BERNARD CYWINSKI**, **JON JACKSON**, Dan Haden, Frank Grauman, William Loose, Randy Reid, Russell Roberts, Karl Backus, and Gregory Mottola. The firm has additional offices in Pittsburgh, Philadelphia, Seattle, and San Francisco. In 1994, the practice received the Architecture Firm Award from the American Institute of Architects and has received over 300 regional, national, and international design awards. Significant work includes Forest House, Cornwall, Connecticut (1975); the Software Engineering Institute, Pittsburgh, Pennsylvania (1987); the Pacific Rim Estate, Medina, Washington (joint venture with Cutler Anderson Architects, 1997); the Headquarters for Pixar Animation Studios, Emeryville, California (2001); and the Liberty Bell Center Independence National Historical Park, Philadelphia, Pennsylvania (2003). Current work includes Williams College Library and Faculty Buildings, Williamstown, Massachusetts; the California Institute of Technology Chemistry Building, Pasadena, California; the Peace Arch U.S. Port of Entry, Blaine, Washington; the Prototype and a series of high-profile retail stores for Apple Computer (various locations worldwide).

# HOUSE AT THE SHAWANGUNKS
## NEW PALTZ, NY
## 2003 - 05

FLOOR AREA: 195 m² (2100 ft.²)
CLIENT: not disclosed
COST: not disclosed
PROJECT TEAM. Peter Bohlin, Lee Clark, Julie Scotchie

The Shawangunk Ridge is a mountain formation considered to be among the best rock climbing sites in the United States. It is located in New York state, extending from the northernmost point of New Jersey to the Catskill Mountains. New Paltz is in Ulster County, 154 kilometers (90 miles) north of New York City. Built on a steeply sloped, wooded site, "the house's cubic volume projects from the hillside against the backdrop of the Shawangunk Ridge. A diagrammatically proportional rectangular volume rises behind the cube, anchoring it to the sloping landscape. The cube's black-stained concrete foundation forms a strong yet unobtrusive pedestal." Red and green-stained cedar siding marks the exterior of the residence, while a single slope roof rises parallel to the hillside. A glass-walled dining area "appears to float among the trees." The double-height living room with its peeled log corner columns also opens broadly into the natural setting. The clients are artists involved in film, graphic design, and jewelry. Not surprisingly, they are also rock climbers.

Die Shawangunk Ridge gilt als eine der besten Felsformationen zum Klettern in den Vereinigten Staaten. Sie liegt im Staat New York und erstreckt sich vom nördlichsten Punkt New Jerseys bis zu den Catskill Mountains. New Paltz liegt im County Ulster, 154 km nördlich von New York City. Der auf steil abschüssigem, bewaldetem Gelände errichtete »kubische Baukörper des Hauses springt vor dem Hintergrund der Shawangunk Ridge aus dem Hang hervor. Ein quaderförmiger Baukörper erhebt sich hinter dem Kubus und verankert ihn in dem abschüssigen Gelände. Das geschwärzte Betonfundament des Kubus fungiert als solider, gleich-

wohl unauffälliger Sockel.« Rot und grün gebeizte Verschalungen aus Zedernholz kennzeichnen das Äußere des Wohnhauses, während die Neigung des durchgehenden Dachs parallel zum Hang verläuft. Der verglaste Essbereich »scheint zwischen den Bäumen zu schweben«. Auch der Wohnraum mit doppelter Geschosshöhe und seinen Eckpfeilern aus entrindeten Baumstämmen öffnet sich weit zur umgebenden Natur. Die Bauherren sind in den Bereichen Film, grafische Gestaltung und Schmuckdesign tätige Künstler; außerdem sind sie natürlich begeisterte Kletterer.

La formation montagneuse de la Shawagunk Ridge est un des meilleurs sites d'alpinisme aux États-Unis. Elle se trouve dans l'État de New York entre la pointe nord du New Jersey et les montagnes des Catskill. New Paltz est situé dans le comté d'Ulster, à 154 km de New York. Édifié sur une pente abrupte, et boisée, « le volume cubique de la maison se projette du flanc de la colline sur le flanc de la Shawagunk Ridge. Un volume sur une base rectangulaire s'élève derrière le cube et l'ancre dans la pente. Les fondations en béton teint en noir forment un socle solide mais discret. » Des bardages en cèdre teinté rouge et vert recouvrent l'extérieur dont les deux volumes sont abrités sous une toiture à une pente, parallèle au terrain. Un espace de repas entouré de murs vitrés « semble flotter dans les arbres ». Le séjour double-hauteur à colonnes d'angles faites de troncs d'arbre s'ouvre tout aussi largement sur l'environnement naturel. Les clients sont des artistes travaillant respectivement dans le cinéma, la création graphique et la joaillerie. Inutile de préciser que ce sont aussi des alpinistes.

As the architects say, "The pristine beauty of this steeply sloped, wooded site called for simple geometry and clean, basic materials." The site map to the right shows the location of the house on its slope.

Den Architekten zufolge verlangte »die unverfälschte Schönheit dieses abschüssigen, bewaldeten Geländes klare Geometrie und schlichte Ausgangsmaterialien«. Der Lageplan rechts verdeutlicht den Standort des Hauses auf dem Abhang.

Pour l'architecte : « La beauté primitive de ce site boisé en forte déclivité appelait une géométrie simple et des matériaux basiques et nets. » À droite, le plan du terrain montre l'implantation de la maison dans la pente.

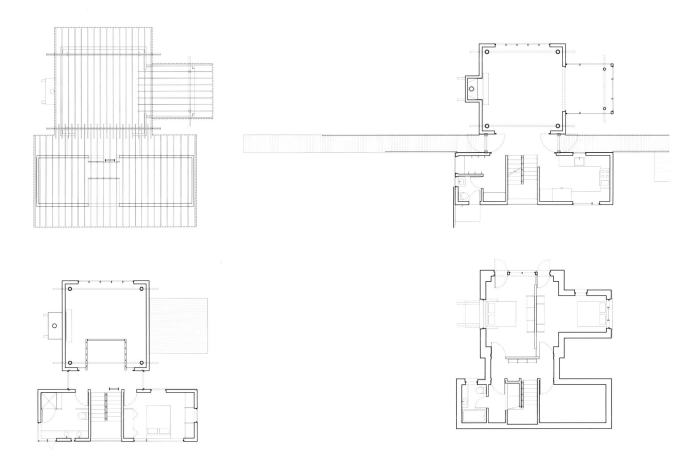

The cedar siding of the house is stained red or green. A single-slope roof recalls the slope of the site and rises parallel to the hillside. The dining room projects from the southwest side of the main cubic volume and "appears to float among the trees."

Die Zedernholzverschalung des Hauses ist rot und grün gebeizt. Die geneigte Dachfläche wiederholt das Gefälle des Geländes und steigt parallel zum Abhang an. Das Esszimmer ragt aus der Südwestseite des kubischen Hauptbaukörpers hervor, dabei »scheint es zwischen den Bäumen zu schweben«.

Le bardage de cèdre est teinté en rouge et vert. Le toit dont le versant unique rappelle la pente du terrain s'élève parallèlement au sol. La salle-à-manger se projette de la façade sud-ouest du cube principal et « semble flotter dans les arbres ».

Brightly colored surfaces and light, modern furniture confirm the significance of the cheerful exterior of the house. The presence of the timber roof and log columns is a constant reminder of the presence of the forest, visible through every window of the house.

Leuchtend farbige Oberflächen und leichte, moderne Möbel unterstreichen das freundliche Äußere. Die Präsenz des Holzdachs und der Pfeiler aus unbehandelten Baumstämmen erinnert an die waldreiche Umgebung, die aus jedem Fenster des Hauses zu sehen ist.

Des surfaces de couleurs vives et un mobilier moderne léger renforcent l'aspect chaleureux de l'extérieur de la maison. Le voligeage en bois et les colonnes en grumes fonctionnent comme un rappel de la présence de la forêt visible de chaque fenêtre de la maison.

For clients who enjoy rock-climbing, the architects expressed an open, "fun-loving" spirit within the house, which retains something of the spirit of a studio in the trees. Polycarbonate sheeting is used along the stairway to bring light to the family room below and the master bedroom and bath above.

Für die kletterbegeisterten Bauherren schufen die Architekten eine offene »fröhliche« Atmosphäre, die etwas vom Geist eines Baumhauses hat. Entlang der Treppe wurde eine Verkleidung aus Polycarbonat verwendet, um Licht in den unten liegenden Mehrzweckraum und in das oben befindliche Elternschlafzimmer und Bad einfallen zu lassen.

Pour leurs clients amateurs d'alpinisme, les architectes ont traité l'intérieur dans un esprit « fun » qui a quelque chose de l'esprit d'une cabane dans un arbre. Les panneaux de polycarbonate de l'escalier permettent de mieux éclairer le séjour multifonctionnel, juste en dessous, et la chambre principale et sa salle de bains au-dessus.

# 3

# BOORA ARCHITECTS

**BOORA ARCHITECTS**
720 SW Washington Street
Suite 800
Portland, Oregon 97205-3510

Tel: +1 503 226 1575
Fax: +1 503 241 7429
e-mail: info@boora.com
Web: www.boora.com

Founded in 1958, Boora Architects plans and designs performing arts centers and museums; campus buildings and master plans; recreation, athletic, and community centers; schools; mixed-use developments; custom homes; offices; and government centers. Notable recent work includes the Mark O. Hatfield United States Courthouse, Portland, Oregon (with Kohn Pederson Fox Associates, 1997); the Clackamas High School, Clackamas, Oregon (2002); the Mondavi Center for the Arts, Davis, California (2002); the Adidas America Corporate Headquarters, Portland, Oregon (2003); the Portland Institute for Contemporary Art Temporary Theater, Portland, Oregon (2004); the National Underground Railroad Freedom Center, Cincinnati, Ohio (with Blackburn Architects, 2004); and the Mesa Arts Center, Mesa, Arizona (2005). Current work includes the Collin County Arts Center, Allen, Texas; the Federal Reserve Bank of San Francisco Pacific Northwest Operations Center, Renton, Washington; the Metropolitan Condominiums, Portland, Oregon; the Stanford University Environment + Energy Building, Palo Alto, California; the University of California, Santa Cruz McHenry Library Renovation and Addition, Santa Cruz, California; and the Virginia Tech University Creative Arts Center and Fine Arts Building, Blacksburg, Virginia.

# TBA FESTIVAL TEMPORARY THEATER
## PORTLAND, OR 2004

FLOOR AREA: 2196 m² (23 638 ft.²)
CLIENT: Portland Institute for Contemporary Art
COST: $10 000

Boora Architects participated in the 2004 and 2005 Time-Based Art (TBA) Festival organized by the Portland Institute for Contemporary Art, described as "an international arts festival programmed with the pioneering performances of contemporary masters and emerging artists who re-frame our contemporary moment in time, offering glimpses of new possibilities through theater, performance, dance, music, and electronic media." In 2004, the institution required a 200-seat theater, a cabaret stage for performances, a bar, and café. A member of the Institute's board provided an empty warehouse for the event, Boora offered their services, and a contractor provided free construction services, allowing the very low budget to be maintained. Out of general concern, the project was developed with "recycled, recyclable, recovered, or resalable materials utilizing design and construction methods that would limit damage to materials and ease construction and dismantling." Using "scaffolding, pegboard, fire-treated (translucent) visqueen, five-gallon plastic buckets, 3/4" MDF board, recycled carpet tiles, plastic zip ties, and fluorescent lights," Boora used the one bay of the warehouse and accommodated the theater area with the existing space, while another group handled the café and bar.

Boora Architects beteiligten sich 2004 und 2005 an dem vom Portland Institute for Contemporary Art veranstalteten Time-Based Art (TBA) Festival, ein »internationales Kunstfestival, zu dessen Programm avantgardistische Darstellungen zeitgenössischer und vor allem aufstrebender Künstler zählen, die sich mit unserer gegenwärtigen Zeit beschäftigen und durch Theater, Performance, Tanz, Musik und elektronische Medien den Blick für neue Möglichkeiten eröffnen«. Im Jahr 2004 benötigte das Institut ein Theater mit 200 Sitzplätzen, eine Kabarettbühne für Performances, eine Bar und ein Café. Ein Kuratoriumsmitglied des Portland Institute stellte ein leerstehendes Lagerhaus zur Verfügung, Boora Architects boten ihre Dienste an, und ein Bauträger stellte die unentgeltliche Bauausführung in Aussicht, alles Faktoren, die es ermöglichten, im Rahmen des äußerst knappen Budgets zu bleiben. Aus Gründen des Umweltschutzes wurde das Projekt mit »aufbereiteten, wieder verwendbaren oder weiterverkäuflichen Materialien ausgeführt; dabei kamen Entwurfs- und Bauverfahren zur Anwendung, die Schaden an Materialien begrenzen und Auf- und Rückbau erleichtern.« Boora verwendete »Gerüstmaterial, Hartfaserplatten, feuerhemmendes (lichtdurchlässiges) Visqueen, knapp 20 l fassende Plastikeimer, 1,2 cm starke mitteldichte Faserplatten, Teppichfliesen aus Recyclingmaterial, Plastikverschlüsse und Leuchtstofflampen« und nutzte den einen Teil der Lagerhalle, um das Theater unterzubringen, während eine andere Gruppe für Café und Bar verantwortlich war.

Boora Architects a participé aux éditions 2004 et 2005 du Time-Based Art (TBA) Festival organisé par le Portland Institute for Contemporary Art, « un festival international d'arts programmant des spectacles d'avant-garde de maîtres contemporains et d'artistes émergents qui recadrent notre passage momentané dans le temps, offrant des aperçus sur les possibilités nouvelles offertes par le théâtre, la performance, la danse, la musique et les médias électroniques. » En 2004, l'institution avait besoin d'une salle de 200 places, d'une scène de type cabaret pour des performances, d'un bar et d'un café. Un membre du conseil d'administration de l'Institut a fourni un entrepôt désaffecté, Boora a offert ses services et un entrepreneur s'est chargé gratuitement des travaux, ce qui a permis de rester dans les limites d'un budget extrêmement serré. Dans un souci écologique, le projet a été réalisé à partir « de matériaux recyclés, recyclables, récupérés ou revendables et à partir de méthodes de conception et de construction qui limitent les dommages causés aux matériaux et facilitent la construction et le démontage. » À grand renfort de « pièces d'échafaudages, panneaux à ficher, panneaux translucides traités anti-feu, seaux en plastique de 20 l, planches d'aggloméré, dalles de moquette recyclées, liens en plastique et tubes fluorescents », Boora a investi une travée de l'entrepôt pour y aménager la salle, un autre groupe se chargeant du café et du bar.

Using five-gallon plastic buckets, scaffolding, and other "recycled, recyclable, recovered, or resalable materials," the architects created a 200-seat temporary theater inside an existing warehouse for the duration of the festival.

Unter Einsatz von Plastikeimern, Gerüstbauteilen und anderen »aufbereiteten, wiederverwendbaren oder weiter verkäuflichen« Materialien schufen die Architekten für die Dauer des Festivals in einem bestehenden Lagerhaus ein Interimstheater mit 200 Plätzen.

À l'aide de cuvettes de plastique de 20 l, d'éléments d'échafaudage et d'autres matériaux « recyclés, recyclables, récupérés ou revendables », les architectes ont créé, pour la durée du festival, une salle temporaire de 200 places dans un entrepôt existant.

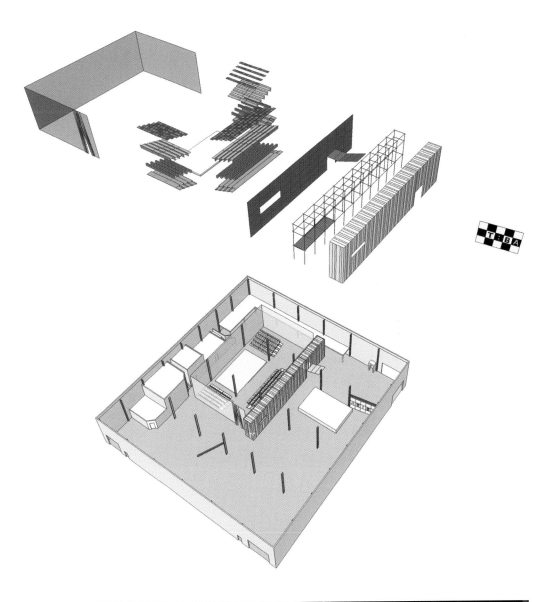

Recycled carpet tiles are used on the risers. As the architects explain, "The team positioned this whole (theater) assembly in front of existing offices lining one wall of the building, whose poor construction warranted concealment for their inconsistency with the qualitative goals for the festival environment."

Auf den Sitzstufen kamen wieder verwendete Teppichfliesen zum Einsatz. Die Architekten zu ihrem Entwurf: »Das Team platzierte diese ganze Theateranlage entlang einer Wand des Gebäudes vor vorhandene Büroräume. Diese mussten aufgrund ihrer schlechten baulichen Qualität, die nicht mit den qualitativen Zielsetzungen des Festivalmilieus vereinbar war, verdeckt werden.«

Des dalles de moquettes recyclées habillent les contremarches. Comme l'expliquent les architectes : « L'équipe a positionné cet assemblage [le théâtre] devant des bureaux existants doublant un mur du bâtiment, dont la pauvreté de construction nécessitait d'être cachée tant elle jurait avec les objectifs qualitatifs de l'environnement de ce festival. »

# TBA FESTIVAL TEMPORARY EVENT COMPLEX PORTLAND, OR 2005

FLOOR AREA: 1800 m² (19 384 ft.²)
CLIENT: Portland Institute for Contemporary Art
COST: $15 000 (estimated)
LANDSCAPE ARCHITECT: Allison K. Rouse

Created for the period between September 9 and September 18, 2005, this installation occupied one square block in an industrial area of Portland's Northwest neighborhood. Temporary scaffold structures housing a beer garden and a common outdoor event space were erected on a large asphalt service yard, while existing buildings lent for the purpose by an artist and property owner housed other events. A former printing press was thus used to create a theater accommodating up to 100 persons, while a warehouse on the other side of the block was transformed into a cabaret for 300 to 500 persons and a restaurant with 80 to 100 seats. Existing office spaces were converted for use as backstage support areas. Relying once again on a number of donations and offers of free services, the Portland Institute for Contemporary Art succeeded in organizing one of the city's premier cultural events for a budget of just $15 000. The involvement of Boora, including hundreds of hours of free design and execution work, represents an explicit acceptance of the fact that architects cannot content themselves with building "timeless" structures for wealthy patrons. The temporary and effervescent nature of this initiative might in a sense be closer to performance art than to architecture in the usual sense, but it underlines the ways in which contemporary architecture has evolved.

Das für die Dauer des Festivals vom 9. bis zum 18. September 2005 errichtete Projekt nahm den Raum eines Häuserkarrees in einem Industriegebiet im Nordwesten von Portland ein. In einem großflächigen, asphaltierten Betriebshof wurden für einen Biergarten behelfsmäßige Gerüstkonstruktionen errichtet, während andere Events in vorhandenen Bauten stattfanden, die der Eigentümer, ein Künstler, leihweise zur Verfügung stellte. So wurde in einer ehemaligen Druckerei ein Theater für bis zu 100 Besucher geschaffen; ein Lagerhaus auf der anderen Seite des Karrees wurde in ein Kabarett für 300 bis 500 Besucher und dazu in ein Restaurant mit 80 bis 100 Plätzen umgewandelt. Vorhandene Büroräume wurden zu Garderoben und für ähnliche Nutzungen umgebaut. Dem Portland Institute for Contemporary Art, dem wiederum eine Reihe von Schenkungen und unentgeltlich angebotene Arbeitsleistungen zugute kamen, gelang es mit einem Budget von gerade 15 000 Dollar, eines der erstrangigen Kulturereignisse der Stadt zu organisieren. Die Beteiligung von Boora, die Hunderte von Entwurfsstunden und ausführende Arbeiten umfasste, belegt eindrucksvoll, dass Architekten sich nicht damit begnügen können, für reiche Auftraggeber »zeitlose« Bauten zu errichten. Der provisorische und spontane Charakter dieser Initiative hat in gewisser Hinsicht mehr mit Performance-Kunst als mit Architektur im traditionellen Sinn gemein, aber sie verdeutlicht die Wege, auf denen sich die zeitgenössische Architektur bewegt.

Cré pour la durée du festival, du 9 au 18 septembre 2005, cette installation occupait un *block* d'une zone industrielle du nord-ouest de Portland. Dans une cour asphaltée, des constructions temporaires en éléments d'échafaudage accueillaient un café de plein air et un espace pour événements extérieurs, tandis que d'autres manifestations se déroulaient dans des bâtiments voisins prêtés pour l'occasion par un artiste propriétaire des lieux. Une ancienne imprimerie ainsi transformée en théâtre de 100 places, et un entrepôt de l'autre côté du block a été en cabaret de 300 à 500 places et restaurant de 80 à 100 couverts. Des bureaux existants ont été aménagés en coulisses. S'appuyant là encore sur un certain nombre de donations et de collaborations gratuites, le Portland Institute of Contemporary Art a réussi à animer l'un des plus importants événements culturels de la ville pour un budget d'à peine 15 000 dollars. L'implication de Boora – des centaines d'heures gratuites de conception et de suivi de chantier – signifie également que des architectes ne peuvent se contenter de construire des projets « intemporels » pour de riches mécènes. La nature temporaire et effervescente de cette entreprise est peut-être en un sens plus proche de l'art de la performance que de l'architecture au sens usuel, mais elle met en lumière les multiples voies empruntées par l'architecture contemporaine.

The architects list their materials as "scaffolding, concert canopy, construction fencing, plywood, Astroturf, outdoor café lighting, synthetic cloth, and paint."

Die Architekten führen ihre Materialien als »Gerüstteile, Konzertbaldachin, Bauzaun, Sperrholz, Astroturf, Café-Außenbeleuchtung, Kunstfasergewebe und Farbe« auf.

La liste des matériaux cités par les architectes comprend : « ... des échafaudages, un auvent pour orchestre, des barrières de chantier, du contreplaqué, de l'astroturf, de l'éclairage extérieur de café, de la toile synthétique et de la peinture. »

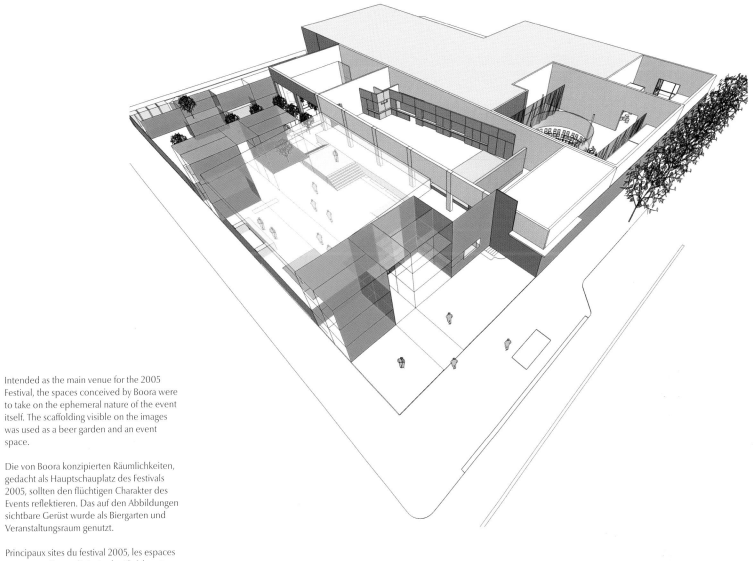

Intended as the main venue for the 2005 Festival, the spaces conceived by Boora were to take on the ephemeral nature of the event itself. The scaffolding visible on the images was used as a beer garden and an event space.

Die von Boora konzipierten Räumlichkeiten, gedacht als Hauptschauplatz des Festivals 2005, sollten den flüchtigen Charakter des Events reflektieren. Das auf den Abbildungen sichtbare Gerüst wurde als Biergarten und Veranstaltungsraum genutzt.

Principaux sites du festival 2005, les espaces conçus par Boora étaient adaptés à la nature éphémère de l'événement. Les échafaudages visibles sur les images servaient à la fois de café en plein air et d'espace pour des mani-festations.

# 4

# DILLER SCOFIDIO + RENFRO

**DILLER SCOFIDIO + RENFRO**
36 Cooper Square 5F
New York, New York 10003

Tel: +1 212 260 7971
Fax: +1 212 260 7924
e-mail: disco@dsrny.com
Web: www.dsrny.com

**ELIZABETH DILLER** was born in Lodz, Poland, in 1954. She received her Bachelor of Architecture degree from the Cooper Union School of Arts in 1979. She is a Professor of Architecture at Princeton University. **RICARDO SCOFIDIO,** born in New York in 1935, graduated from the Cooper Union School of Architecture and Columbia University, where he is currently a Professor of Architecture. They founded Diller+Scofidio in 1979. **CHARLES RENFRO** became a partner in 2004. Renfro was born in Houston, Texas, in 1964. He graduated from Rice University and Columbia, where he taught for three years. DS+R works today with a permanent staff of 40. According to their own description, "DS+R is a collaborative, interdisciplinary studio involved in architecture, the visual arts and the performing arts. The team is primarily involved in thematically-driven experimental works that take the form of architectural commissions, temporary installations and permanent site-specific installations, multi-media theater, electronic media, and print." They recently completed Facsimile, a permanent media installation for the San Francisco Arts Commission at the Moscone Convention Center (2004); the Blur Building Expo 02, Yverdon-les-Bains, Switzerland (2000–02); and the Viewing Platforms at Ground Zero in Manhattan. Other works include the Brasserie, Seagram Building, New York (1998–99); Slither, a social housing building, Gifu (Japan) Jet Lag, a multi-media work for the stage in collaboration with The Builders Association; two dance collaborations with the Lyon Ballet Opera of France and Charleroi/Danses of Belgium, both currently touring the U.S., Europe, and Asia. Current work includes the Lincoln Center projects including the expansion of Juilliard School of Music and a renovation of Alice Tully Hall; the redevelopment of Tivoli Gardens in Copenhagen, Denmark; the conversion of the High Line, a 2.4 kilometer (1.5 miles) stretch of elevated railroad into a New York City park; the Institute of Contemporary Art in Boston, Massachusetts, which is currently under construction; and collaborations with the Wooster Group and the filmmaker Mira Nair.

# MOTT STREET TOWNHOUSE NEW YORK, NY 2006 - 07

FLOOR AREA: 892 m² (9600 ft.²)
CLIENT: not disclosed
COST: not disclosed
PROJECT LEADER: Stefan Röschert

This seven-story apartment building is located on a deep, narrow site between two existing tenement buildings in the NoLIta area of Manhattan, north of St. Patrick's Old Cathedral, which is at the corner of Mott and Prince Streets. The two lower floors are given over to retail space, with two duplexes, and another "floor-through" apartment above. One of the most interesting aspects of the architecture in this instance is the challenge posed to the architects by local historic district zoning restrictions. They were required to use masonry as the primary building material for the façade. The architects solution was to veil the glass curtain wall facing east with "a system of operable, glass masonry screens. A running bond of glass bricks threaded together by rods like beads on a necklace are suspended on tracks at every floor slab in front of the floor-to-ceiling glass wall. The screen can be drawn by the tenants like grand mineral curtains." This system allowed them both to meet regulations and to bring light into the building, while creating an interesting interplay between the views into and out of the building. The architects conclude that "The façade inverts the Semperian notion of 'Stoffwechsel' by weaving rigid building units into a flaccid and heavy textile."

Das siebengeschossige Appartementhaus steht in Manhattan auf einem tiefen, schmalen Grundstück zwischen zwei vorhandenen Wohnhäusern in NoLIta (North of Little Italy), nördlich von St. Patrick's Old Cathedral an der Ecke von Mott und Prince Street. Die beiden unteren Geschosse sind für Ladengeschäfte vorgesehen, während darüber zwei Maisonettewohnungen und ein weiteres Appartement geplant sind. Einer der interessantesten Aspekte der Architektur ist in diesem Fall die Herausforderung, die die Auflagen des Denkmalschutzes stellten. Als Baumaterial für die Fassade musste in erster Linie Mauerwerk verwendet werden. Die Lösung bestand darin, die nach Osten gelegene, vorgehängte Glaswand mit einem »System aus beweglichen gläsernen Mauerwerkelementen zu verkleiden.

Ein Läuferverband von Glasbausteinen, die wie Perlen an einer Halskette auf Stäbe aufgefädelt sind, hängt an jeder Grundplatte auf Schienen vor der deckenhohen Glaswand. Die Mauerwerkselemente lassen sich von den Bewohnern wie großgeratene, mineralische Vorhänge bewegen.« Dieses System wurde einerseits den Vorschriften gerecht und brachte andererseits Licht in das Gebäude. Darüber hinaus ergab sich eine interessante Wechselwirkung zwischen den Blicken in das Gebäude und aus ihm heraus. Abschließend bemerken die Architekten, dass »die Fassade die Semper'sche Vorstellung des ›Stoffwechsels‹ umkehrt, indem starre Bauteile mit einem beweglichen, gleichwohl gewichtigen Textil verwoben werden.«

Cet immeuble d'habitation de sept étages se dresse sur un terrain long et étroit pris entre deux immeubles locatifs dans le quartiers de NoLIta à Manhattan, au nord de la cathédrale Saint-Patrick et à l'angle des rues Mott et Prince. Les deux niveaux inférieurs sont réservés au commerce de détail. Au-dessus sont aménagés deux duplex et un appartement « transversal ». L'un des aspects les plus intéressants de ce projet est le défi posé aux architectes par le règlement d'urbanisme dans ce quartier historique, qui exigeait une façade en maçonnerie. Leur solution a été de tendre le mur rideau côté est « d'un système d'écrans en maçonnerie de verre mobile. Des panneaux formés de briques de verre solidarisées par des tiges de métal, à la manière de perles sur un collier, coulissent dans des rails accrochés en nez de dalle devant la paroi vitrée sur toute la hauteur des pièces. Les occupants peuvent faire glisser ces écrans minéraux comme des rideaux » Ce système a permis à la fois de se plier à la réglementation et de faire pénétrer davantage de lumière dans les lieux tout en créant un jeu intéressant de transparences dans les deux sens. Pour les architectes, « la façade inverse la notion issue de Semper du *Stoffwechsel* en faisant d'éléments constructifs rigides un textile lourd et mobile ».

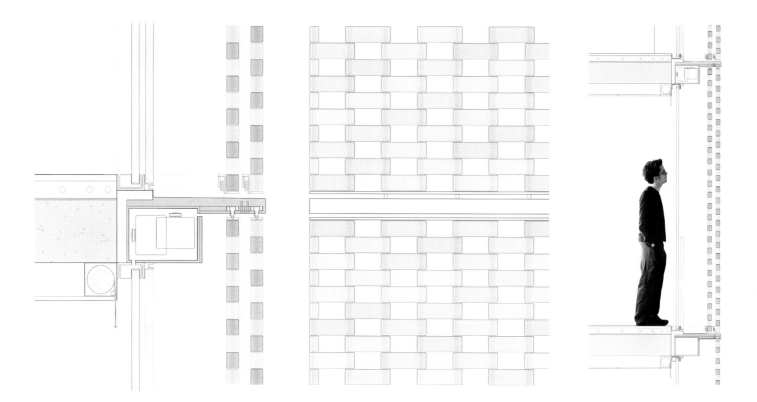

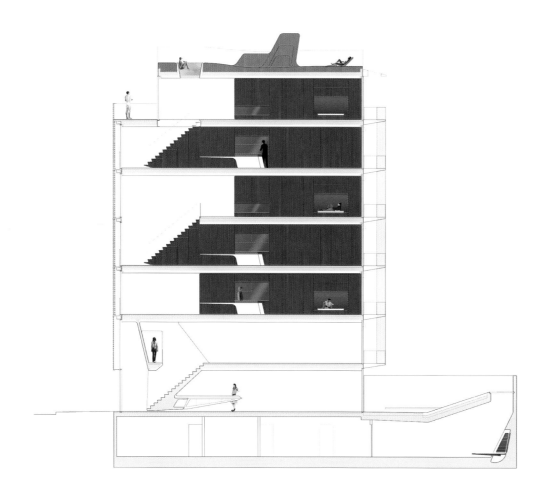

Above, a detailed drawing of the woven glass brick façade invented by the architects to satisfy building requirements calling for a masonry surface. The building contains retail spaces below, and two duplexes topped by a full-floor residence.

Oben eine Detailzeichnung der Fassade aus Glassteingewebe, mit der die Architekten den Bauvorschriften entsprachen, die Mauerwerk vorsahen. Das Gebäude enthält im unteren Teil Ladengeschäfte, darüber zwei Maisonettewohnungen sowie ein weiteres Appartement.

Ci-dessus, dessin de détail du « tissage » du mur de verre en façade inventé par les architectes pour répondre à la réglementation qui demandait un plan en maçonnerie. Le bâtiment contient des espaces commerciaux en bas et deux duplex ainsi qu'un appartement sur un seul niveau.

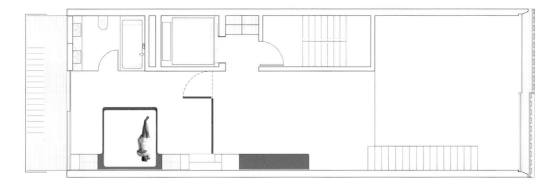

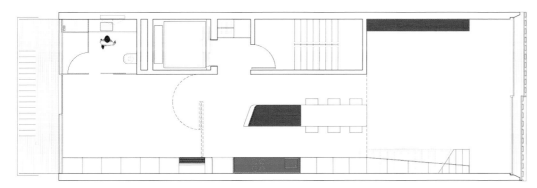

Floor plans and a drawing show the continuity of the space in the duplex apartments, leading to the floor-to-ceiling glass wall with its operable screens that can be "drawn by the tenants like grand mineral curtains."

Geschossgrundrisse und eine Zeichnung zeigen die räumliche Kontinuität in den Maisonettewohnungen, die zu der deckenhohen Glaswand mit ihren beweglichen Elementen führt, »die von den Bewohnern wie großflächige mineralische Vorhänge geöffnet und geschlossen werden können«.

Les plans et la visualisation montrent le continuum spatial jusqu'au mur de verre toute hauteur à éléments mobiles qui peuvent être « tirés par les occupants comme un magnifique rideau minéral ».

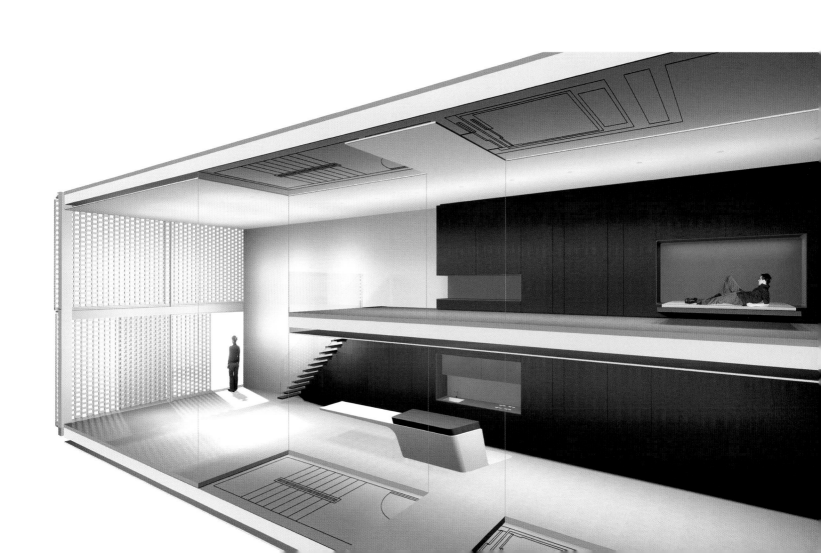

# FACSIMILE
# SAN FRANCISCO, CA
# 2004

AREA: 24.3 meter-tall steel frame, 4.5 x 7.6 meter LED video screen
CLIENT: San Francisco Arts Commission COST: $2 million
PROJECT LEADER: Matthew Johnson

This unusual art project is actually quite typical of the activities of Liz Diller and Ricardo Scofidio, who are known as much for their installations as they are for their architecture. Mounted on the glass façade of the Moscone Convention Center in San Francisco, Facsimile is intended to move along the surface of the building while it broadcasts a combination of live video feeds from the second-level lobby of the Center, randomly interspersed with fictional prerecorded programs showing office, hotel, or lobby activity. The architects explain, "Thus, actual building occupants and actual interior spaces are confused with pre-recorded impostors. As such, the apparatus could be seen as a scanning device, a magnifying lens, a periscope (a camera at a high elevation looks toward the city), and as an instrument of deception substituting impostors for actual building occupants and spaces." An interesting commentary on a culture that seems to thrive on "reality" TV and art that comes closer and closer to everyday life, Facsimile has posed some technical problems, but certainly remains a challenge to those who would arbitrarily define the limits that separate art and architecture.

Das ungewöhnliche Kunstprojekt ist eigentlich recht typisch für die Aktivitäten von Liz Diller und Ricardo Scofidio, die gleichermaßen für ihre Installationen bekannt sind wie für ihre Architektur. Das auf der Glasfassade des Moscone Convention Centers in San Francisco angebrachte »Facsimile« soll sich entlang der Oberfläche des Gebäudes bewegen und Videomaterial senden, das in der Lobby auf der zweiten Ebene des Centers aufgenommen wird. Darin wahllos eingestreut sind fiktive, vorab aufgenommene Programme, die Tätigkeiten aus Büro, Hotel oder Lobby zeigen. Den Architekten zufolge werden »so tatsächliche Bewohner des Gebäudes und wirkliche Innenräume mit vorher aufgenommenen Eindringlin-gen durcheinander gebracht. So gesehen könnte man die Apparatur als Scanner, als Lupe, als Periskop (eine Kamera in großer Höhe schaut auf die Stadt) und als Instrument der Täuschung ansehen, das Hochstapler gegen wirkliche Bewohner des Gebäudes und der Räume austauscht.« »Facsimile« ist ein interessanter Kommentar zu einer Kultur, die sich mit Reality-TV anscheinend prächtig gedeiht, und einer Kunst, die sich dem täglichen Leben immer weiter annähert. Das Projekt wirft zwar einige technische Probleme auf, bleibt aber sicherlich eine Herausforderung für all jene, die die Grenzen zwischen Kunst und Architektur willkürlich ziehen möchten.

Étonnant, ce projet artistique reste cependant caractéristique des activités de Liz Diller et Ricardo Scofidio, tous deux aussi connus pour leurs installations que pour leur architecture. Monté sur la façade de verre du Moscone Convention Center à San Francisco, Facsimile se déplace parallèlement à celle-ci tout en diffusant un montage de prises de vue vidéo en direct du hall du second niveau du centre, entrecoupé de manière aléatoire d'éléments de programmes de fiction montrant l'activité des bureaux de l'hôtel ou du hall. « Ainsi, expliquent les architectes, les occupants réels de l'immeuble et les volumes intérieurs réels sont mélangés à des « imposteurs » préenregistrés. Ce dispositif peut être considéré comme un scanner, une loupe, un périscope (une caméra fixée en partie supérieure filme la ville) et un instrument de duperie substituant les imposteurs aux occupants et aux espaces réels du bâtiment. » Commentaire intéressant sur une culture dans laquelle la télé-réalité triomphe et l'art se rapproche de plus en plus de la vie quotidienne, Facsimile a posé certains problèmes techniques mais reste un intéressant défi lancé à ceux qui veulent tracer arbitrairement des frontières entre l'art et l'architecture.

As the giant screen travels across the surface of the building, on some occasions, live interior pictures are projected, and at other moments, "fictional, pre-recorded video programs that appear to be live are randomly substituted."

Während sich der riesige Schirm über die Gebäudeoberfläche bewegt, sind darauf entweder Livebilder aus dem Inneren zu sehen oder »fiktive, vorab aufgenommene Videoprogramme mit der Anmutung von Livematerial.«

Des images prises en direct de l'intérieur du bâtiment sont diffusées sur l'écran géant qui se déplace sur la façade de l'immeuble. À certains moments s'y « substituent des programmes vidéo de fiction préenregistrés qui semblent pris en direct. »

# FRANK O. GEHRY

**GEHRY PARTNERS, LLP**
12541 Beatrice Street
Los Angeles, California 90066

Tel: +1 310 482 3000
Fax: +1 310 482 3006
e-mail: info@foga.com

Born in Toronto, Canada, in 1929, **FRANK O. GEHRY** studied at the University of Southern California, Los Angeles (1949–54), and city planning at Harvard (1956–57). Principal of Frank O. Gehry and Associates, Inc. (now Gehry Partners, LLP), in Los Angeles, since 1962, today employing up to 140 people, he received the 1989 Pritzker Prize. Some of his notable projects are the Loyola Law School, Los Angeles, California (1978–97); the Norton Residence, Venice, California (1982–84); the California Aerospace Museum, Los Angeles (1982–84); the Schnabel Residence, Brentwood, California (1986–89); the Festival Disney, Marne-la-Vallée (1989–92); the Vitra Furniture Museum and Factory, Weil-am-Rhein (1987–89) and the firm's headquarters, Basel (1988–94); the Frederick R. Weisman Art Museum at the University of Minnesota, Minneapolis (1990–93); The Guggenheim Museum, Bilbao (1991–97); and the Experience Music Project, Seattle, Washington (1995–2000). Recent work includes the DZ Bank Headquarters, Berlin (1995–2001); the Fisher Center for the Performing Arts at Bard College, Annandale-on-Hudson, New York (1998–2003); Walt Disney Concert Hall, Los Angeles (1987–2003); and the Massachusetts Institute of Technology Stata Complex, Cambridge, Massachusetts (1998–2004). Current work includes the Hotel at Marques de Riscal, Elciego, Spain; the Ohr-O'Keefe Museums, Biloxi, Mississippi; the InterActiveCorp Headquarters, New York, New York; the Atlantic Yards, Brooklyn, New York; the New World Symphony, Miami, Florida; and the Theatre for a New Audience, Brooklyn, New York.

# JAY PRITZKER PAVILION MILLENNIUM PARK

## CHICAGO, IL 2001 - 04

FLOOR AREA: 3344 m² (36 000 ft.²) building; 8617 m² (92 750 ft.²) lawn
HIGHT: 36.6 meters (120 ft.) CLIENT: Millennium Park COST: not disclosed
ARCHITECT: Gehry Partners, LLP DESIGN PARTNER: Frank O. Gehry
PROJECT DESIGNER: Craig Webb
PROJECT ARCHITECT: Manoucher Eslami

Opened in July 2004, the Millennium Park was one of the most significant combinations of art, architecture, and landscape design to be completed in the United States in many years. Aside from Gehry's Pritzker Pavilion published here, the Crown Fountain by artist Jaume Plensa; the contemporary Lurie Garden designed by the team of Kathryn Gustafson, Piet Oudolf, and Robert Israel; and Anish Kapoor's "Cloud Gate" sculpture on the AT&T Plaza are all part of the project. The 36-meter-high (120-foot-high) billowing structure made of stainless-steel ribbons with its accompanying trellis of steel pipes is one of Gehry's freest and, in some ways, most successful projects. With 4000 fixed seats and accommodation for 7000 more, the outdoor concert venue quickly became a new symbol of Chicago. As Gehry states the goal, "How do you make everyone—not just the people in the seats, but the people sitting 121 meters (400 feet) away on the lawn—feel good about coming to this place to listen to music? And the answer is, you bring them into it. You make the proscenium larger; you build a trellis with a distributed sound system. You make people feel part of the experience." The trellis, in the shape of a flattened dome, is constructed of curved steel pipes typically spaced 65 feet (20 meters) apart. The trellis is supported by cylindrical concrete pylons clad in stainless steel panels." Set on top of a three-level underground parking structure and bus and rail lines, it can be said that the Pavilion concentrates urban experience in an artistic style for which Gehry has become justifiably famous.

Bei dem im Juli 2004 eröffneten Millennium Park handelt es sich um eine der bedeutendsten Kombinationen von Kunst, Architektur und Landschaftsgestaltung, die in den Vereinigten Staaten seit Jahren verwirklicht wurden. Abgesehen von dem hier vorgestellten Pritzker Pavilion sind auch der Crown Fountain des Künstlers Jaume Plensa, der vom Team Kathryn Gustafson, Piet Oudolf und Robert Israel gestaltete Lurie Garden sowie Anish Kapoors Skulptur »Cloud Gate« auf der AT&T Plaza Bestandteil des Projekts. Die mehr als 36 m hohe wogende Struktur aus Edelstahlbändern und dem dazugehörigen Gitter aus Stahlrohren ist eines von Gehrys unabhängigsten und in mancher Hinsicht erfolgreichsten Projekten. Mit seinen 4000 fest eingebauten Sitzplätzen und Raum für weitere 7000 Besucher wurde dieser Ort für Open-Air-Konzerte rasch zu einem neuen Symbol Chicagos.

Gehry über das Projekt: »Wie schafft man es, dass sich alle – nicht nur die Leute auf den Sitzplätzen, sondern auch die, die rund 120 m weit weg auf dem Rasen sitzen, freuen, hierher gekommen zu sein, um Musik zu hören? Man muss sie einbeziehen. Man vergrößert die Vorderbühne und baut ein Gitter mit einer darauf verteilten Lautsprecheranlage. Die Leute sollen sich als Teil des Erlebnisses fühlen.« Das Gitter in Form einer abgeflachten Kuppel ist aus gebogenen Stahlrohren zusammengesetzt, die im Abstand von 20 m nebeneinander stehen. Es wird von runden Betonpylonen getragen, die mit Edelstahlplatten ummantelt sind." Der über einer dreigeschossigen Tiefgarage sowie Bus- und Bahnlinien stehende Pavillon verdichtet urbanes Erleben in einem Stil, für den Gehry mit Recht berühmt ist.

Ouvert en juillet 2004, le Millenium Park est l'une des plus significatifs ensembles de créations artistiques, architecturales et de paysage initié aux États-Unis depuis de nombreuses années. En dehors du Pritzker Pavilion de Frank Gehry publié ici, on y trouve la Crown Fountain de l'artiste Jaume Plensa (NDT : it's Plensa not Plena I suppose), le Lurie Garden, jardin contemporain conçu par l'équipe Kathryn Gustafson, Piet Oudolf et Robert Israel, et le Cloud Gate, sculpture de Anish Kapoor installée sur la AT&T Plaza. Le pavillon est une structure en rubans d'acier qui culmine à 36 m, accompagnée d'un treillis en tubes d'acier. C'est l'une des réalisations les plus libres et d'une certaine façon les plus réussies de Gehry. L'auditorium de plein air de 4000 places assises fixes et 7000 places libres supplémentaires est rapidement devenu un des symboles de Chicago. Gehry précise ainsi son objectif : "Comment faire pour que chacun, et non seulement les gens assis sur des sièges, mais ceux qui sont assis sur le gazon à 120 m de la scène, se sentent à l'aise pour écouter de la musique? La réponse est : faites les pénétrer dans la musique. Vous faites une scène plus grande, vous construisez un treillis qui soutient un système de diffusion du son. Vous donnez aux gens le sentiment de faire partie du spectacle." Le treillis, en forme de voûte plate, est en tubes d'acier incurvés espacés de 20 m. Il est soutenu par des pylônes cylindriques en béton habillés de panneaux en acier inoxydable." Posé sur un parking souterrain de trois niveaux et au-dessus des lignes de bus et de rail, ce pavillon concentre une globalité de l'expérience urbaine dans le style qui a rendu à juste titre l'architecte célèbre.

As opposed to the modernist blocks in the background, Gehry's Pavilion takes a much freer, almost sculptural form, which looks all the more animated in contrast to the city's buildings. A large sculpture by Anish Kapoor, "Cloud Gate", is visible to the left of the picture above.

Im Gegensatz zu den modernistischen Blocks im Hintergrund nimmt Gehrys Pavillon eine viel freiere, plastische Form an, die gerade verglichen mit den städtischen Bauten umso lebensvoller wirkt. Auf dem Bild links oben ist Anish Kapoors große Skulptur »Cloud Gate« zu sehen.

La forme sculpturale et libre du pavillon de Gehry semble d'autant plus animée qu'elle contraste avec celle des tours modernistes visibles dans le lointain. Une importante sculpture d'Anish Kapoor, « Cloud Gate », est visible sur la photographie ci-dessus, à gauche.

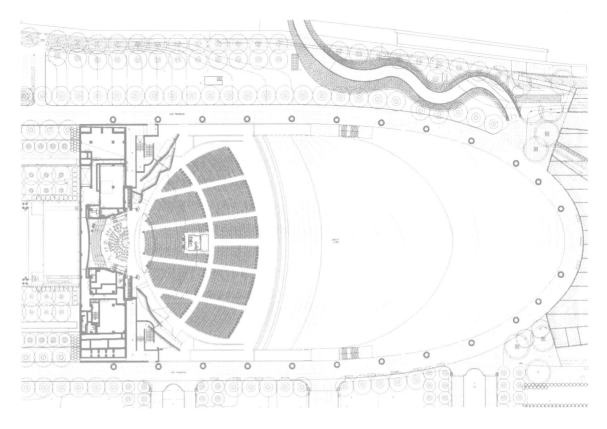

The ovoid plan is occupied only in part by the billowing shapes of the main Pavilion, while the radiating lines in the plan above, also visible in the photo below, are a trellis with an integrated sound system.

Drei eiförmige Grundriss wird nur zum Teil von den wogenden Formen des Hauptpavillons überspannt, während Bogenlinien ein Gitter mit integriertem Tonsystem bilden, wie im Grundriss und auch auf dem Foto unten zu erkennen ist.

Le plan ovoïde n'est occupé qu'en partie par les volumes ondulés du pavillon principal. Les lignes en courbe qui figurent sur le plan ci-dessus et se retrouvent dans la photo ci-dessous représentent le treillis métallique supportant le système de sonorisation.

# 6

# STEVEN HOLL

**STEVEN HOLL ARCHITECTS, P.C.**
450 West 31st Street
11th floor
New York, New York 10001

Tel: +1 212 629 7262
Fax: +1 212 629 7312
e-mail: mail@stevenholl.com
Web: www.stevenholl.com

Born in 1947 in Bremerton, Washington, **STEVEN HOLL** obtained his Bachelor of Architecture degree from the University of Washington (1970). He studied in Rome and at the Architectural Association (AA) in London (1976). He began his career in California and opened his own office in New York in 1976. The office presently works with a staff of 35. Holl has taught since 1981 at Columbia University. His notable buildings include the Hybrid Building, Seaside, Florida (1984–88); the Void Space/Hinged Space, Housing, Nexus World, Fukuoka, Japan (1989–91); the Stretto House, Dallas, Texas (1989–92); the Makuhari Housing, Chiba, Japan (1992–97); the Chapel of St. Ignatius, Seattle University, Seattle, Washington (1994–97); the Kiasma Museum of Contemporary Art, Helsinki, Finland (1993–98); an extension of the Cranbrook Institute of Science, Bloomfield Hills, Michigan (1996–99); the Sarphatistraat offices in Amsterdam (2000); and dormitories at MIT, Cambridge, Massachusetts (2002). Steven Holl recently completed the Bellevue Art Museum, Bellevue, Washington, and an expansion and renovation of the Nelson Atkins Museum of Art, Kansas City, Missouri (opening spring 2007). Other current work includes the Knut Hamsun Museum, Hamaroy, Norway; an Art and Art History Building for the University of Iowa, Iowa City, Iowa; and the College of Architecture at Cornell University, Ithaca, New York (2004). He recently won the competition for the Knokke-Heist Casino in Belgium and completed the Pratt Institute Higgen Hall Center Wing in Brooklyn. Steven Holl is also working on a new residence at the Swiss Embassy in Washington, D.C.; the Cité du Surf et de l'Océan in Biarritz, France; the Denver Justice Center Courthouse (in collaboration with Klipp Architecture, Denver); and the Herming Center of the Arts in Denmark. Currently under construction are the Linked Hybrid, Beijing, China, and the Art & Architecture Museum, Nanjing, China.

# TURBULENCE HOUSE
# ABIQUIU, NM
# 2001-04

FLOOR AREA: 84 m² (900 ft.²) CLIENT: Richard Tuttle
COST: not disclosed PRINCIPAL: Steven Holl
PROJECT ARCHITECT: Anderson Lee PROJECT COORDINATOR: Richard Tobias, AIA
PROJECT TEAM: Arnault Biou, Matt Johnson

This house is unusual in many respects. Its form was generated with three-dimensional or parametric models and its 30-panel aluminum-sheet skin was manufactured by A. Zahner and Co. in Kansas City according to the computer specifications furnished by the architect. The New Mexico house, set on a windswept desert mesa (a mesa—Spanish for "table"—is an elevated area of land with a flat top and sides that are usually steep cliffs) was "imagined like the tip of an iceberg indicating a much larger form below, allows turbulent wind to blow through the center." Although intended for the sculptor Richard Tuttle, the Turbulence House has an exact twin in a sculpture park in Schio, Italy, created for an exhibition in Vicenza in 2003 and moved thereafter. 6.7 meters (22 feet) high at its tallest point, the house has a kitchen, dining, and living space on the ground floor, with a study, sleeping area, and bathroom above. Poured-in-place concrete is used on the ground floor and rough pine on the upper level. Photovoltaic roof panels are used to provide some electricity that powers heat pumps. The light color of the aluminum and the fact that most window surfaces face north allows the house to remain relatively cool in the summer months. The importance of this house lies in the fact that it is both sculptural and technically advanced, having been created with the latest 3-D techniques, proving that technology and an artistic sensibility can indeed be combined in contemporary architecture.

Dieses Haus ist in vieler Hinsicht ungewöhnlich. Seine Form entstand mithilfe dreidimensionaler oder parametrischer Modelle, und seine aus 30 Tafeln zusammengesetzte Außenhaut aus Aluminiumblech wurde von A. Zahner and Co. in Kansas City nach den vom Architekten gelieferten Computerangaben angefertigt. Dieses in New Mexico auf einer windgepeitschten Wüstenmesa stehende Haus (mesa, das spanische Wort für Tisch, bezeichnet ein erhöhtes, flaches Gelände, das in der Regel von steilen Felswänden begrenzt wird), das »in der Vorstellung als Spitze eines Eisbergs existierte, die eine weit größere, darunterliegende Form anzeigt, lässt ungestüme Winde durch seine Mitte fegen«. Obgleich es für den Bildhauer Richard Tuttle vorgesehen war, gibt es ein exaktes Duplikat des Hauses, das 2003 für eine Ausstellung in Vicenza entstand und anschließend in einen Skulpturenpark im italienischen Schio versetzt wurde. Das an seinem höchsten Punkt 6,7 m hohe Haus verfügt im Erdgeschoss über eine Küche sowie einen Ess- und Wohnraum, darüber befindet sich ein Arbeitszimmer, der Schlafbereich und ein Bad. Für das Parterre wurde Ortbeton, für das obere Stockwerk unbehandeltes Kiefernholz verwendet. Auf dem Dach befindliche Fotovoltaikzellen erzeugen die Energie, mit der Wärmepumpen betrieben werden. Die helle Farbe des Aluminiums und der Umstand, dass die meisten Fenster nach Norden zeigen, lassen das Haus in den Sommermonaten verhältnismäßig kühl bleiben. Die Bedeutung dieses Hauses liegt darin, dass es sowohl plastisch wie technisch fortschrittlich ist, da es mittels der neuesten 3-D-Verfahren konzipiert wurde; es ist Beleg dafür, dass Technik und künstlerisches Empfinden sich in zeitgenössischer Architektur sehr wohl vereinen lassen.

Cette maison surprend à de nombreux égards. Sa forme est issue de modèles paramétriques ou en trois dimensions et sa peau constituée de 30 panneaux de tôle d'aluminium a été fabriquée par A. Zahner and Co. de Kansas City selon des spécifications directement fournies par l'ordinateur de l'architecte. Cette maison située sur une mesa désertique balayée par les vents (une mesa, table en espagnol, est un plateau surélevé dont les côtés sont généralement des falaises) a « été imaginée comme le sommet d'un iceberg qui laisse deviner une forme beaucoup plus importante en dessous ; elle laisse les turbulences du vent pénétrer dans sa partie centrale. » Bien que créée pour le sculpteur Richard Tuttle, elle possède sa jumelle exacte installée dans un parc de sculptures à Schio en Italie, construite pour une exposition organisée à Vicence en 2003. D'une hauteur de 6,7 m à son point le plus élevé, elle comporte une cuisine, un séjour/salle-à-manger au rez-de-chaussée, ainsi qu'un bureau, une zone réservée au sommeil et à l'étage une salle de bains. Le sol du rez-de-chaussée est en béton coulé, celui de l'étage en pin. Sur le toit, des panneaux photovoltaïques alimentent des pompes à chaleur. La couleur claire de l'aluminium et l'orientation nord de la plupart des fenêtres permettent Hent de maintenir une certaine fraîcheur à l'intérieur pendant les mois d'été. L'importance de ce projet tient au couplage de sa qualité sculpturale et de techniques d'avant-garde, grâce aux plus récentes approches de la conception en trois dimensions. Il montre que l'architecture contemporaine peut marier technologie et sensibilité artistique.

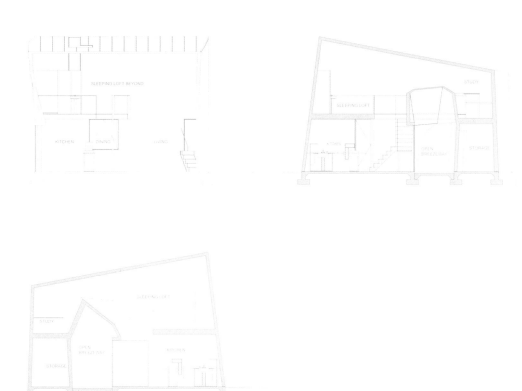

Produced by A. Zahner and Co., a Kansas City sheet metal fabrication company that utilizes digital definition combined with craftsmanship to produce highly intricate metal shapes and forms, the metal skin of the house is its defining exterior feature.

A. Zahner and Co., eine in Kansas City ansässige Firma für Feinbleche, produzierte die Metallverkleidung des Hauses, die sein Äußeres prägt. Die Firma verbindet digitale Präzision mit Handwerkskunst, um hochkomplexe Metallformen herzustellen.

Due à A. Zahner and Co., une entreprise de Kansas City spécialisée dans les constructions en tôle métallique, la peau métallique de la maison définit sa forme. L'entreprise allie la précision des outils informatiques à un savoir-faire artisanal pour produire des formes d'une complexité élevée.

Although it is close to adobe houses built by Richard Tuttle, the Turbulence House appears in the image below to sit alone on the snow-covered New Mexican desert mesa. As the architect explains, "Its form, imagined like the tip of an iceberg indicating a much larger form below, allows turbulent wind to blow through the center."

Obgleich es sich in der Nähe des von Richard Tuttle erbauten Adobe House befindet, steht das Turbulence House scheinbar allein auf der schneebedeckten Wüstenmesa. Der Architekt führt dazu aus: »Dieses Haus, das in der Vorstellung als Spitze eines Eisbergs existierte, die eine weit größere, darunterliegende Form anzeigt, lässt ungestüme Winde durch seine Mitte fegen.«

Proche des maisons en adobe de Richard Tuttle, la Turbulence House semble isolée au sommet de sa *mesa* enneigée. Comme l'explique l'architecte : « Sa forme, imaginée comme le sommet d'un iceberg qui laisse deviner une forme beaucoup plus importante en dessous; elle laisse les turbulences du vent pénétrer dans sa partie centrale. »

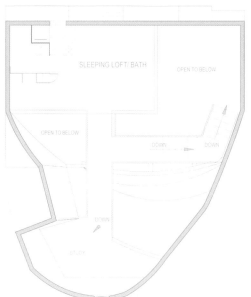

KITCHEN   DINING   LIVING   UP   STORAGE

SLEEPING LOFT/ BATH   OPEN TO BELOW   OPEN TO BELOW   DOWN   DOWN   DOWN   STUDY

The simplicity of the furnishings of the house allows its metal stairway and ramp to stand out together with the unusually rich interior forms. Although sculptural in its exterior appearance, the house is carefully thought out as a habitable space.

Die schlichte Möblierung des Hauses lässt die Metalltreppe und Rampe sowie die ungewöhnlich prächtigen Innenformen zur Geltung kommen. Das von Außen plastisch wirkende Haus bietet im Inneren einen wohl durchdachten, bewohnbaren Raum.

La simplicité du mobilier met en valeur l'escalier et la rampe métalliques ainsi que la volumétrie étonnement riche de l'intérieur. D'aspect extérieur sculptural, cette maison offre cependant un volume habitable parfaitement pensé.

The clear, waxed poured-in-place concrete ground floor and simple column give way to a simple geometrically defined kitchen area in the image above. Steven Holl's great sensitivity to light and the subtleties of color appears in these interior images.

Der aus Ortbeton gegossene, farblos gewachste Fußboden und ein schmuckloser Pfeiler leiten in einen schlichten, geometrisch abgegrenzten Küchenbereich über. Steven Holls hoch entwickeltes Empfinden für Licht und farbliche Abstufungen kommt auf diesen Abbildungen des Innenraums zur Geltung.

Ci-dessus, le sol en béton ciré et une colonne toute simple délimitent l'espace de la cuisine de composition strictement géométrique. La grande sensibilité de Steven Holl à la lumière et aux dégradés de couleurs est manifeste dans ces vues de l'intérieur.

# THE SWISS RESIDENCE
## WASHINGTON, D.C.
## 2001 - 06

FLOOR AREA: 2640 m² CLIENT: Swiss Federal Office for Building and Logistics
COST: not disclosed ARCHITECTS: Steven Holl Architects, Rüssli Architekten AG
DESIGN ARCHITECTS: Steven Holl and Justin Rüssli
ASSOCIATES IN CHARGE, SHA: Stephen O'Dell, Tim Bade
PROJECT ARCHITECT, SHA: Olaf Schmidt
PROJECT ARCHITECT, RA: Mimi Kueh

Completed in September 2006, the new Residence of the Swiss Embassy in Washington, D.C., was designed by Steven Holl and the Swiss firm Rüssli Architects. They won the project in a competition held in 2001 in which ten other teams participated. Located on a hill with a view of the Washington Monument, the residence contains two formal dining rooms, three salons, one reception hall, and a stone terrace. The Ambassador's living quarters, two guest rooms, and staff areas are located on the upper floor. According to the architects, "The materiality of the residence is an important feature of the design. The building's charcoal color concrete and sand-blasted translucent structural glass planks were inspired by the black rocks and white snow of the Swiss Alps. The floors are made of black terrazzo and dark stained bamboo, a highly renewable resource." The building was designed to the strict Swiss "Minergie" standards intended to keep energy consumption low.  This interesting collaboration succeeds in keeping something of the Swiss taste for a certain minimalism in architecture while also playing on the layered complexity and mastery of light that is typical of the work of Steven Holl. Intended for a large number of events that will attract numerous visitors, the Residence will certainly be a worthy representative of Switzerland, while also underlining the close relationship with the host country, surely an ideal combination in these circumstances.

Die im September 2006 fertig gestellte, neue Residenz der Schweizer Botschaft in Washington, D.C., ist ein Entwurf von Steven Holl und dem Schweizer Büro von Rüssli Architects. Die Architekten erhielten den Auftrag, nachdem sie einen 2001 ausgeschriebenen Wettbewerb, an dem sich zehn weitere Teams beteiligt hatten, für sich entscheiden konnten. Die auf einem Hügel mit Blick auf das Washington Monument gelegene Residenz umfasst zwei offizielle Speisezimmer, drei Salons, eine Empfangshalle und eine steinerne Terrasse. Die Wohnräume des Botschafters, zwei Gästezimmer und die Räume der Bediensteten befinden sich im Obergeschoss. Den Architekten zufolge stellen »die bei dem Projekt verwendeten Werkstoffe ein wichtiges Merkmal des Entwurfs dar. Der anthrazitfarbene Beton und das sandgestrahlte, lichtdurchlässige Strukturglas sind vom schwarzen Fels und weißen Schnee der Schweizer Alpen inspiriert. Die Fußböden bestehen aus schwarzem Terrazzo und schwarz gebeiztem Bambus, einem in hohem Grade regenerativem Material.« Der Entwurf des Gebäudes richtet sich nach den strengen Schweizer »Minergi«- Normen zur Reduzierung des Energieverbrauchs. Dieser interessanten Partnerschaft gelingt es, etwas von der Schweizer Neigung zu einem gewissen Minimalismus in der Architektur zu erhalten, während sie geschickt die für das Schaffen Steven Holls typische Vielschichtigkeit und Beherrschung von Licht nutzt. Die Residenz, die bei vielen Gelegenheiten Gäste empfangen soll, wird mit Sicherheit die Schweiz würdig repräsentieren, während sie gleichzeitig die enge Beziehung zum Gastland unterstreicht, eine unter diesen Umständen gewiss ideale Kombination.

Achevée en septembre 2006, la nouvelle résidence de l'ambassadeur de Suisse à Washington a été conçue par Steven Holl et l'agence suisse Rüssli Architects, lauréats d'un concours organisé en 2001, auquel dix autres équipes avaient participé. Située sur une colline dominant le Washington Monument, cette résidence comprend deux salles à manger officielles, trois salons, une salle de réception et une terrasse. Les appartements de l'ambassadeur, deux chambres d'amis et celles du personnel occupent l'étage. Selon le descriptif des architectes : « La matérialité de cette résidence est une des caractéristiques importantes de ce projet. La teinte charbon de bois du béton et les panneaux de verre structurel translucide sablé sont inspirés des roches noires et de la neige des Alpes. Les sols sont en terrazzo noir et en bambou teinté foncé, matériau hautement écologique. » L'ensemble répond aux normes strictes de la réglementation suisse Minergie visant à réduire au maximum la consommation énergétique. Cette équipe à la composition intéressante a su marier le goût suisse pour un certain minimalisme avec la multiplicité des niveaux de lecture et la maîtrise de la lumière typiques de l'œuvre de Steven Holl. Prévue pour recevoir des manifestations publiques, la résidence représentera certainement très bien la Suisse, tout en cultivant une relation étroite avec son pays hôte, combinaison idéale en l'occurrence.

An iridescent simplicity reigns in these images of the Swiss Residence, where the strict geometric volumes are reflected in the pond. The austerity that is indeed typical of Swiss contemporary architecture, here meets in a felicitous way with Steven Holl's sense of light and volume.

Diese Ansichten der Schweizer Botschaft, deren streng geometrische Baukörper sich im Wasser spiegeln, zeichnen sich durch strahlende Schlichtheit aus. Die in der Tat für die zeitgenössische Architektur der Schweiz typische Nüchternheit wird hier aufs Glücklichste durch Steven Holls Gespür für Licht und Volumina ergänzt.

Une simplicité iridescente règne dans ces images de la résidence de l'ambassadeur suisse où l'on voit la stricte géométrie des volumes se refléter dans le bassin. La rencontre de l'austérité typique de l'architecture suisse contemporaine et du sens de la lumière et des volumes de Steven Holl se révèle particulièrement heureuse.

The use of sandblasted, translucent, structural glass planks on the exterior is unexpected and certainly contributes to the subtle elegance of the surface. Whereas the forms and lines of the architecture are clean and simple, the glass gives a slightly undefined appearance to the whole. The rectilinear plan resists the slightly diagonal form of the site.

Die Verwendung von sandgestrahlten, lichtdurchlässigen Paneelen aus Strukturglas am Außenbau überrascht und trägt sicherlich zur Raffinesse der Oberfläche bei. Während Linienführung und Formen der Architektur klar und einfach sind, verleiht das Glas dem Ganzen ein etwas unbestimmtes Erscheinungsbild. Der gradlinige Grundriss lässt sich nicht auf die leicht diagonale Form des Baugeländes ein.

Inattendue, l'utilisation de panneaux de verre structurel sablé translucide pour l'extérieur contribue à la subtilité de l'aspect des surfaces. Si les formes et les lignes de l'architecture sont simples et nettes, le verre leur confère un caractère quelque peu indéfinissable. Le plan en croix se heurte pour ainsi dire au tracé légèrement en biais du terrain.

Steven Holl's watercolors of the interior not only envisage the furniture to be used, but also take into account works of art. As is the case in the view of the stairway to the right, the watercolors reveal a complex interplay of transparency and opacity, as well as a deft use of light.

Auf seinen aquarellierten Ansichten des Interieurs deutet Steven Holl nicht nur die zu verwendende Möblierung an, sondern berücksichtigt auch die Ausstattung mit Kunstwerken. Wie im Fall der Treppenansicht rechts offenbaren die Aquarelle ein komplexes Wechselspiel von Transparenz und Opazität, ebenso wie den gekonnten Umgang mit Licht.

Les aquarelles de Steven Holl pour l'intérieur donnent des indications pour l'aménagement intérieur, qu'il s'agisse du mobilier on des œuvres d'art. Comme le montre la vue de l'escalier à droite, ces aquarelles révèlent un jeu complexe de transparence et d'opacité ainsi qu'une utilisation habile de la lumière.

# 7

# MICHAEL JANTZEN

MICHAEL JANTZEN
27800 N. McBean Parkway
Suite 319
Valencia, California 91354

Tel: +1 310 989 1897
e-mail: mjantzen@yahoo.com
Web: www.humanshelter.org

In 1971, **MICHAEL JANTZEN** received a Bachelor's degree with a major in fine arts from Southern Illinois University (Edwardsville, Illinois). In 1973, he received a Master of Fine Arts degree with a major in Multimedia from Washington University (St. Louis, Missouri). Jantzen was then hired by Washington University's School of Fine Arts and by the School of Architecture, to teach studio courses as a visiting professor. In 1975, one of his first solar houses was featured in numerous national and international magazines. Over the next ten years, he continued to design and build energy-efficient structures with an emphasis on modular high-tech housing systems. In 1997, he was awarded a grant from Art Center College of Design Digital Media Department to develop ideas for an interface between media and architecture. In 1998, Jantzen developed several digital media projects that were published widely. He created a conceptual house called the Malibu Video Beach House, and Elements, an interactive digital media theme park. From 1999 to 2001, he designed and built the M house, "a modular, relocatable, environmentally responsive, alternative housing system." Since then Jantzen has worked with various companies as a consultant to develop concepts for many experimental design projects. Some of these projects include a foldable fabric vacation house, a series of interactive media-based bus stops, a transformable glass-and-steel pedestrian footbridge, and a design study for a modular workplace environment. In addition, Jantzen has developed a line of fabric-based transformable furniture, lighting, and environments for the commercial market. In 2005, Jantzen began to work on low-cost eco-friendly steel housing systems and a number of modular, prefabricated, transformable pavilions.

# CONCEPT WINERY
## 2005

FLOOR AREA: 612 m² (6588 ft.²)
CLIENT: none
COST: not determined

"I'm rethinking the whole notion of living space," said Michael Jantzen in describing his surprising M-House (Gorman, California, 2000). In many ways that modular concept house prefigured the esthetic and practical aspects of Jantzen's most recent scheme, a winery that as yet has neither a client nor a location. "Conceptually," he says, "this design is based on my vision of a symbolic abstraction of a giant grape vine that grows up from the earth onto a trellis to function as a new kind of truly organic winery." And like the leaves of the real grape vine, this symbolic abstraction can also produce its own power from the sun. To be created, like the M-House, from a system of "modular, re-arrangeable, sustainable building components, the Winery, at least in its original version, would be approximately 9 meters (30 feet) tall, 18 meters (60 feet) wide, and 34 meters (112 feet) long. The green curved panels of the structure would be covered with a thin photovoltaic coating "which allows the surface of the structure to produce its own electrical energy." The modular trellis would be made, according to Jantzen, out of Corten steel. This element, as well as fundamentals such as the size, color, or form of the overall structure could be changed to suit any client's needs. Architects as well-known, as Frank O. Gehry, Steven Holl, Herzog & de Meuron, or Santiago Calatrava have engaged in the design of wineries; Jantzen in many respects proposes a more radical rereading of the requirements of such facilities, offering both modernity and sustainability.

»Ich überdenke die ganze Vorstellung von Wohnraum«, erläuterte Michael Jantzen bei der Beschreibung seines 2000 entstandenen M-House in Gorman, Kalifornien. In vieler Hinsicht nimmt dieses Haus mit seiner Modulbauweise die ästhetischen und praktischen Aspekte von Jantzens neuestem Projekt vorweg, eine Weinkellerei, für die es weder einen Auftraggeber noch einen Standort gibt. »Vom Konzept her«, sagt er, »basiert dieser Entwurf einer wahrhaft organischen Weinkellerei auf meiner Vision der symbolischen Abstraktion eines riesigen Weinstocks, der aus dem Boden an einem Spalier emporwächst.« Und wie das Laub eines wirklichen Weinstocks kann diese symbolische Abstraktion mithilfe der Sonne ihre eigene Energie erzeugen. Wie das M-House soll die Kellerei aus einem System »modularer, umgruppierbarer, nachhaltiger Bauelemente« bestehen und zumindest in ihrer ursprünglichen Version etwa 9 m hoch, 18 m breit und 34 m lang sein. Die grünen, gebogenen Paneele des Gebäudes sollen mit einem dünnen fotovoltaischen Überzug beschichtet werden, so dass »das Gebäude mit der Oberfläche seinen eigenen Strom produziert«. Das aus Modulen zusammengesetzte Spalier würde Jantzen zufolge aus Corten-Stahl gefertigt. Dieses Element könnte, ebenso wie Größe, Farbe oder Form des gesamten Bauwerks, nach den Wünschen eines jeden Auftraggebers verändert werden. Verglichen mit Weinkellereien, die namhafte Architekten wie Frank Gehry, Steven Holl, Herzog & de Meuron oder Santiago Calatrava gestalteten, schlägt Jantzen in vieler Hinsicht ein radikaleres Umdenken hinsichtlich der Erfordernisse einer solchen Einrichtung vor und bietet Modernität und Nachhaltigkeit.

« Je suis en train de repenser la notion complète d'espace de vie », annonce Michael Jantzen en décrivant sa surprenante M-House (Gorman, Californie). Sous de nombreux aspects, cette maison-concept modulaire préfigure l'esthétique et les aspects pratiques de son plus récent projet, un chai qui n'a encore trouvé ni son client ni son site. « Conceptuellement, dit-il, ce projet repose sur ma vision d'une stylisation symbolique d'une grappe de raisin géante poussée sur une treille. Il constitue une nouvelle approche de chai authentiquement organique. Comme les feuilles de vigne, cette abstraction peut également produire sa propre énergie à partir du soleil. Devant être construit comme la M-House à l'aide d'un système »d'éléments de construction modulaires, évolutifs et respectueux de l'environnement, ce chai, du moins dans sa version proposée, mesure environ 9 m de haut, 18 de large et 34 de long. Les panneaux verts incurvés seraient recouverts d'un film de cellules photovoltaïques « qui permettent à la structure de produire sa propre énergie électrique ». Le treillis modulaire serait en acier Corten. Cet élément ainsi que les aspects de base comme les dimensions, la couleur ou même la forme générale peuvent varier en fonction des besoins du client. Des architectes aussi prestigieux que Frank Gehry, Steven Holl, Herzog & de Meuron ou Santiago Calatrava se sont mesurés à la problématique du chai, mais Jantzen propose une relecture plus radicale des contraintes de ce type d'installation en leur apportant à la fois la modernité et une dimension écologique.

The curved green colored panels are covered with a thin film photovoltaic coating that "allows the surface of the structure to produce its own electrical energy." The panels are formed into two different radii, some insulated and used to enclose spaces that need to be heated or cooled, others un-insulated and used to shade spaces below the trellis.

Die grünen, gebogenen Paneele des Gebäudes sind mit einem dünnen fotovoltaischen Überzug beschichtet, der eine eigene Stromversorgung ermöglicht. Die Paneele sind zu zwei verschiedenen Krümmungen gebogen; einige sind isoliert und umgeben Räume, die erwärmt oder gekühlt werden müssen, andere bleiben ungedämmt und dienen dazu, Flächen unter dem Spalier zu beschatten.

Les panneaux verts incurvés sont recouverts d'un film de cellules photovoltaïques qui permet à la structure de produire sa propre énergie électrique. Les panneaux ont été formés selon deux courbes différentes. Certains sont isolés et servent à clore les espaces qui ont besoin d'être chauffés ou rafraîchis, d'autres, non-isolants, abritent du soleil les espaces sous le treillis.

# 8

# JONES, PARTNERS: ARCHITECTURE

**JONES, PARTNERS: ARCHITECTURE**
141 Nevada Street
El Segundo, California 90245

Tel: +1 310 414 0761
Fax: +1 310 414 0765
e-mail: info@jonespartners.com
Web: www.jonespartners.com

WES JONES, born in 1958 in Santa Monica, attended the United States Military Academy at West Point, the University of California at Berkeley (B. Arch., 1980), and the Harvard Graduate School of Design, where he received a Master of Architecture degree (1983). A recipient of the Rome Prize in Architecture, he has taught at Harvard, Princeton, IIT, Ohio and Columbia Universities. He is presently teaching at the Southern California Institute of Architecture (SCI-Arc). He worked with Eisenman/Robertson, Architects in New York before becoming partner in charge of design at Holt Hinshaw Pfau Jones in San Francisco. He founded his own practice, Jones, Partners: Architecture, in 1993. DOUG JACKSON, born in 1970 in Hampton (Virginia), attended Virginia Tech (B. Arch. 1993) and Princeton University (M. Arch. 2000) before becoming a partner in 2003. Recent projects include duplex residences in Silverlake and Redondo Beach, single-family residences in Manhattan Beach, Hollywood, Agua Dulce (all California), and Phoenix, Arizona; offices in Carson, California, and Culver City, California; the Book Concern Building apartments in San Francisco, California; a telecom co-location facility in Bahrain, and a host of PRO/con (container) projects in Arcata, Venice, and Culver City, California, and on Molokai, Hawaii.

# SILVERLAKE DUPLEX
# SILVERLAKE, CA
# 2003

FLOOR AREA: 260 m² (2800 ft.²)
CLIENT: Jean Young Jones
COST: $450 000

Built on two previously vacant lots sloping up from Hyperion Avenue, this duplex residence includes two bedrooms set on top of parking space, with an open living/dining/kitchen area above. The two bedrooms are connected by a space the architects call a "swing room" that can be used either to enlarge one of the bedrooms, as an office, or even an extra bedroom. The rather humorous text of the architect explains this project as follows, "The Silverlake Duplex is conceived as an affordable but spacious version of a "chic" urban live/work environment that might appeal to younger professionals, once termed yuppies, but now lower expectations and more edge have turned them into slacker/hackers. In particular, this audience is being dispossessed of its traditional home on the westside (Santa Monica) by rising land values and being forced to relocate inland. Silverlake is a destination of choice for these refugees, combining an urban grittiness with lower prices and more rural topography. Signs of this migration include new restaurants and art gallery/coffee houses, tattoo parlors, and instances of 'interesting' architecture." The upper loft space features a 4.9 x 9.1 meter (16 x 30 feet) window-wall facing the slope side to minimize noise from the busy avenue. Bridges lead from the upper level to a yard behind the house. Steel sunshade louvers, exposed duct-work, and mechanical equipment are concentrated here, while "the remainder of the structure is finished with extreme simplicity and restraint."

Zu diesem Doppelhaus, das auf zwei von der Hyperion Avenue ansteigen-den, zuvor unbebauten Grundstücken errichtet wurde, gehören jeweils zwei Schlafräume, die über einem Parkplatz liegen; darüber gibt es einen offenen Wohn-, Ess- und Küchenbereich. Die beiden Schlafzimmer sind durch einen Raum verbunden, den der Architekt als »Pendelraum« bezeichnet, der entweder zur Erweiterung eines der Schlafzimmer, als Arbeitszimmer oder sogar als zusätz-licher Schlafraum genutzt werden kann. Der eher spaßige Text des Architekten er-läutert das Projekt wie folgt: »Das Silverlake-Doppelhaus ist als erschwingliche, gleichwohl geräumige Unterart eines ›schicken‹, urbanen Wohn-/Arbeitsumfelds konzipiert, das jüngeren Akademikern gefallen könnte, die man einst Yuppies nannte, die sich aber inzwischen aufgrund gesunkener Erwartungen und gestiegener Nervosität in ziellos agierende Computerfreaks verwandelt haben. Insbesondere hat dieses Publikum aufgrund steigender Grundstückspreise seine traditionelle Heimstatt im Westen (Santa Monica) verloren und ist gezwungen, ins Landesin-

nere umzusiedeln. Silverlake ist ein bevorzugter Ort für diese Vertriebenen, da er urbanes Flair mit moderateren Preisen und eher ländlicher Topografie vereint. Zu den Anzeichen dieser Wanderbewegung gehören neue Restaurants und Kunstga-lerien/Cafés, Tätowierstudios und einzelne Fälle von ›interessanter‹ Architektur.« Der obere Raum ist mit einer 4,9 x 9,1 m großen Fensterwand ausgestattet, die an der Hangseite liegt, um den Lärm von der vielbefahrenen Avenue zu mindern. Aus der oberen Ebene führen Brücken in einen hinter dem Haus liegenden Hof. Hier konzentrieren sich stählerne Sonnenschutzblenden, freiliegende Kanalleitungen und technische Einrichtungen, während »das übrige Gebäude mit äußerster Schlichtheit und Zurückhaltung behandelt wurde«.

Construites sur deux parcelles au pied d'une pente de terrain dominant Hy-perion Avenue, ces maisons mitoyennes comprennent chacune deux chambres au-dessus d'un garage, surmontées d'une zone séjour-repas-cuisine ouverte. Les deux chambres sont reliées par un espace que les architectes appellent « swing room » (pièce fluctuante) qui peut servir à agrandir l'une des chambres ou tenir lieu de bureau ou même de chambre supplémentaire. Le texte de présentation as-sez humoristique explique ainsi ce projet : « Le Silverlake Duplex est conçu com-me une version spacieuse mais abordable d'un cadre urbain de vie/travail « chic » susceptible de plaire à ces jeunes membres des professions libérales qui ont dû revoir leurs prétentions à la baisse face à la concurrence et sont devenus des tra-vailleurs à domicile rivés à leurs ordinateurs. Ce public, en particulier, a été chasé de son fief traditionnel côté ouest (Santa Monica) par la spéculation foncière et forcé de se replier vers l'intérieur. Silverlake est une destination de choix pour ces réfugiés car elle offre une topographie plus rurale à des prix abordables. Les signes de cette migration comprennent de nouveaux restaurants, des cafés-galeries d'art, des studio de tatouage et des bribes d'architecture « intéressante. » Le loft en par-tie supérieure présente un mur de verre de 4,9 x 9,1 m face à la pente pour échap-per au bruit de l'avenue très fréquentée. Des passerelles conduisent de ce niveau vers une cour à l'arrière de la maison. Des persiennes en acier, des conduites et des équipements techniques laissés apparents sont concentrés de ce côté tandis que « le reste de la construction est aménagé avec une simplicité et une retenue extrêmes ».

As the sections and elevation below show, the façades of the building on Hyperion Avenue (above) are intentionally quite closed in order to reduce noise levels inside the building, while a glazed façade on the rear brings in light.

Wie Schnitte und Aufriss oben zeigen, sind die Fassaden des Gebäudes an der Hyperion Avenue bewusst recht geschlossen gehalten, um den Lärmpegel im Inneren zu mindern, während die rückseitige Glasfassade Licht einfallen lässt.

Comme le montrent les coupes et l'élévation ci-dessous, les façades de ce petit immeuble donnant sur Hyperion Avenue (ci-dessus) sont volontairement assez fermées pour réduire les inconvénients du bruit. La lumière pénètre par la façade vitrée à l'arrière.

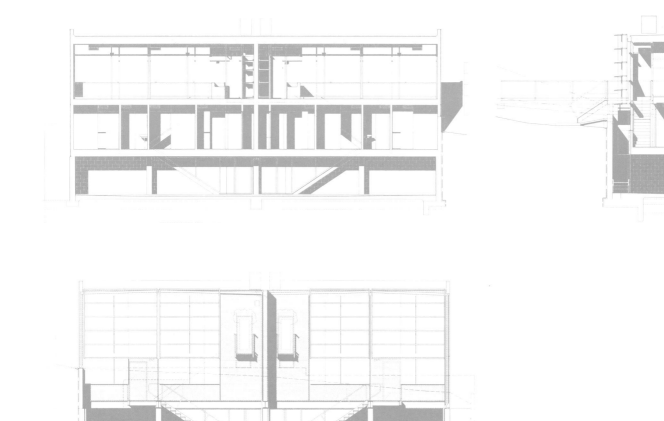

The glazed rear façade at nightfall—showing a decided contrast with the closed street-front façade, and an openness that is more typical of California architecture.

Die rückseitige Glasfassade bei Nacht – hier zeigt sich ein deutlicher Kontrast zur geschlossenen Straßenseite sowie eine für kalifornische Architektur typische Offenheit.

À la tombée de la nuit, la façade arrière entièrement vitrée, image familière de l'architecture californienne, affiche un contraste marqué avec la façade sur rue.

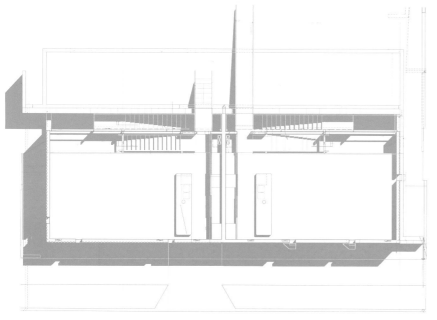

On the rear, glazed side of the building, the architects have concentrated "steel sunshade louvers, stairs and guardrail wall system, sliding wall panels, exposed ductwork and mechanical equipment." The interior architecture is characterized by its "extreme simplicity and restraint."

An der Rückseite des Gebäudes konzentrierten die Architekten »stählerne Sonnenschutzblenden, Treppen und Geländer, verschiebbare Wandpaneele und technische Einrichtungen«. Die Innengestaltung zeigt »äußerste Schlichtheit und Zurückhaltung«.

Sur la partie arrière vitrée, les architectes ont regroupé « des persiennes en acier, les escaliers, le système de garde-corps, des murs coulissants, les tuyauteries apparentes et les équipements techniques. » L'architecture intérieure se caractérise par sa « retenue et sa simplicité extrêmes ».

Since views from the house are concentrated to the rear, the architect writes, "By its arrangement in the building, an explicit critique of humanity's position in the world is embodied: nature in the backyard is literally viewed through a dense screen of mediating technology."

Da sich Ausblicke aus dem Haus auf die Rückseite konzentrieren, schreibt der Architekt: »In der Anordnung [der Technik] ist eine deutliche Kritik an der Position der Menschheit in der Welt enthalten: Die Natur im Hinterhof wird buchstäblich durch eine dichte Schicht Technologie gefiltert.«

Sur la concentration des ouvertures sur l'arrière, l'architecte a pu écrire que « cette disposition de l'immeuble incarne une critique explicite de la position de l'humanité dans le monde : la nature se perçoit vers l'arrière littéralement à travers un écran serré de technologie médiatrice.»

# 9

# LTL
# LEWIS.
# TSURUMAKI.
# LEWIS

**LTL ARCHITECTS**
147 Essex Street
New York, New York 10002

Tel: +1 212 505 5955
Fax: +1 212 505 1648
e-mail: office@LTLwork.net
Web: www.LTLarchitects.com

PAUL LEWIS received his Master of Architecture degree, from Princeton University in 1992, and studied previously at Wesleyan University (B.A. 1988). He is a principal and founding partner of Lewis.Tsurumaki.Lewis, created in 1993. He was an associate at Diller + Scofidio, New York (1993-97). MARC TSURUMAKI received his Master of Architecture degree from Princeton in 1991, after attending college at the University of Virginia. He worked as a project architect in the office of Joel Sanders in New York (1991-97) prior to creating Lewis.Tsurumaki.Lewis. DAVID J. LEWIS completed his architectural studies at Princeton in 1995 after attending Cornell and Carleton College. He was the Publications Director, Cornell University, College of Architecture, Art, and Planning (1997-98). He worked at Peter Guggenheimer, Architects, PPC, New York, as an assistant (1995-96) and in the office of Daniel Libeskind in Berlin (1993) before creating LTL. The firm's recent built projects include the Bornhuetter Hall, Wooster, Ohio (2004); Tides Restaurant, New York, New York (2005); Figge Residence, Wooster, Ohio (2004); Xing Restaurant, New York, New York (2005); Dash Dogs Restaurant, New York, New York (2005); and the Ini Ani Coffee Shop, New York, New York (2004). Current projects include the Arthouse at the Jones Center Renovation and Expansion, Austin, Texas (2005); Vegas888 Spa, Las Vegas, Nevada (2005); Alexakos Townhouse, New York, New York (2005-); Brown Univ. Bio-Medical Center Renovation, Providence, Rhode Island (2005); HPD Housing, East New York, New York (2006); Nazareth House, Allentown, Pennsylvania (2006); West Avenue Live/Work Building, Miami Beach, Florida (2005-); and the Burns Townhouse, Philadelphia, Pennsylvania (2006).

# XING RESTAURANT
## NEW YORK, NY
## 2004 - 05

FLOOR AREA: 186 m² (2000 ft.²)
CLIENT: Michael Lagudis and Chow Down Mgt. Inc.
COST: not disclosed

Located at 785 Ninth Avenue in Manhattan, Xing is a Chinese restaurant located in a residential building whose lightwells posed a particular problem for the layout of the space. As the architects explain, "Employing a logic derived from the Surrealists' game of the Exquisite Corpse, the space is composed of four distinct, yet interlocked areas, each defined by a specific material. The transition of materials moves from hard at the most public (stone and bamboo) to soft at the most private (velvet)." The front bar is clad in layered stone. A corridor is lined with 3000 linear meters of stacked 0.2 inches wide, 2 inches deep acrylic that extends forward into the front dining area, which is otherwise defined by the use of bambooo. In the rear, red velvet panels complete the transition from hard to soft imagined by the architects. Though LTL is now taking on larger projects, they have certainly made a name for themselves with numerous relatively small New York restaurant spaces, each one more inventive and unexpected than the next.

Das chinesische Restaurant Xing befindet sich an der Ninth Avenue 785 in New York in einem Wohnhaus, dessen Lichtschächte bei der Aufteilung des Raums besondere Probleme bereiteten. Die Architekten berichten, sie hätten »einer vom Spiel der Surrealisten ›Le Cadavre Exquis‹ abgeleiteten Logik folgend den Raum in vier unterschiedliche, gleichwohl ineinander greifende Bereiche unterteilt, die sich jeweils durch ein bestimmtes Material auszeichnen. Dabei bewegen sich die Materialien von hart (Stein und Bambus) im mehr öffentlichen bis weich (Samt) im eher privaten Bereich.« Die vordere Bar ist mit geschichtetem Stein verkleidet, ein Korridor mit 3000 laufenden Metern aus 0,6 cm breitem, 5 cm starkem Schichtacryl verschalt, das sich bis in den vorderen Gastraum fortsetzt, in dem ansonsten viel Bambus verwendet wurde. Im hinteren Teil vervollständigen Fliesen aus rotem Samt den von den Architekten geplanten Übergang von hart zu weich. Obgleich LTL inzwischen größere Projekte übernimmt, genießt das Büro seit langem einen guten Ruf in der Gestaltung zahlreicher, eher kleiner New Yorker Restaurants, von denen eines einfallsreicher und überraschender ist als das andere.

Situé 785 Ninth Avenue à Manhattan, Xing est un restaurant chinois installé dans un immeuble résidentiel dont les puits de lumière posaient un problème délicat d'aménagement de l'espace. Comme l'expliquent les architectes : « À partir d'une logique dérivée du jeu surréaliste des cadavres exquis, l'espace se compose de quatre zones distinctes mais imbriquées, chacune définie par un matériau qui lui est propre. La transition entre ces matériaux va du dur, pour les zones les plus ouvertes au public (pierre et bambou), au mou pour les zones les plus privées (velours). » Le bar de l'avant est habillé de plaques rectangulaires de pierre. Le corridor, doublé de 3000 mètres linéaires de petites plaques d'acrylique de 0,6 cm de large et 5 cm d'épaisseur, s'étend jusqu'à la première salle-à-manger définie par le lambrissage en bambou. Dans la partie arrière, des panneaux en velours rouge complètent la transition du dur au mou. Bien que l'agence LTL soit maintenant chargée de projets plus importants, elle s'est fait un nom dans l'univers d'un certain type de restaurants new yorkais tous plus inventifs et plus surprenants les uns que les autres.

The narrow floor plan with its central "bottle-neck" is navigated by the architects using different materials for each space—a layered acrylic ceiling, stone, bamboo, or red velvet. Recessed lighting is "embedded" into the materials "to tease out the richness and depth of the architectural surfaces."

Der schmale Grundriss mit seinem mittigen »Engpass« wird von den Architekten durch die Verwendung unterschiedlicher Materialien für jeden Raum gegliedert – Schichtacryl, Stein, Bambus und roter Samt. Versenkte Beleuchtungskörper sind in die Materialien »eingebettet«, »um Fülle und Tiefe der architektonischen Oberflächen zur Geltung zu bringen«.

L'étroit plan au sol à « étranglement » central est mis à profit par les architectes au moyen de matériaux diversifiés en fonction de chaque volume : plafond en acrylique, pierre, bambou ou velours rouge. L'éclairage dissimulé est « incrusté » dans les matériaux « pour calmer la richesse et la profondeur des surfaces architecturées ».

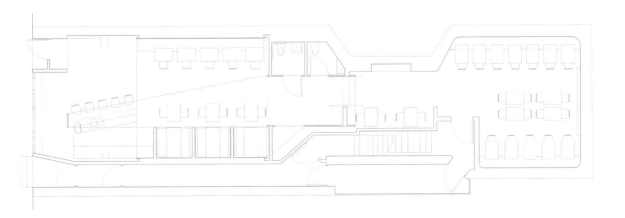

# ARTHOUSE AT THE JONES CENTER
## AUSTIN, TX
## 2005-07

FLOOR AREA: 2230 m² (24 000 ft.²)
CLIENT: Arthouse at the Jones Center
COST: not disclosed

This is a renovation and expansion of an existing contemporary art space adapted from a turn-of-the-century theater and a 1950s department store. According to the architects, "LTL sought to amplify this accumulation of history, by conceiving of the design as a series of integrated tactical additions. The principal charge of the project was to generate a building that would promote excitement about contemporary art, both within the galleries and within the city." One of their most visible gestures is to increase the "porosity" of the building surface by piercing the structure with green laminated glass blocks. Protruding from the exterior, these blocks bring light into the building. The street side façade has been opened and glazed, again for reasons of interior lighting. The main gallery space on the second floor was not turned into a traditional museum area by the architects who preferred to leave the exposed brick walls and open steel trusses visible in the double-height space. Sliding display walls have permitted the architects to preserve the rough character of the existing building. A wooden stairway descends from the roof to the ground floor. With a combination of "green" space and wood, the roof provides an ideal location in the warm climate for dinners, movie screenings, or further art exhibitions, visible from surrounding buildings.

Bei diesem Projekt geht es um die Renovierung und Erweiterung einer bestehenden Räumlichkeit für zeitgenössische Kunst, die aus einem Theater der Jahrhundertwende und einem Kaufhaus aus den 1950er Jahren entstanden ist. Den Architekten zufolge »wollte LTL diese Ansammlung von Historie vergrößern und stellte sich dabei den Entwurf als eine Reihe integrierter, taktischer Anbauten vor. Die Hauptaufgabe des Projekts bestand darin, ein Gebäude zu erstellen, das sowohl in seinen Räumen wie in der Stadt den Enthusiasmus für zeitgenössische Kunst befördern sollte.« Eine der augenfälligsten Maßnahmen besteht darin, die »Durchlässigkeit« des Objekts zu erhöhen, indem man den Baukörper mit Steinen aus grünem Verbundglas »durchbohrte«. Die aus der Wand nach Außen ragenden Steine bringen Licht in den Innenraum. Außerdem wurde die Straßenfassade geöffnet und verglast, um mehr Tageslicht in den Raum holen. Der Hauptausstellungsraum im zweiten Stock wurde von den Architekten nicht zu einer traditionellen Museumsgalerie umgebaut, sondern sie beließen in dem Raum mit doppelter Geschosshöhe die unverputzten Backsteinwände und offenliegenden Stahlbinder. Dank verschiebbarer Schauwände konnten die Architekten den rustikalen Charakter des bestehenden Gebäudes bewahren. Eine Holztreppe führt vom Dach zum Parterre herab. Mit seiner Kombination aus Begrünung und Holz stellt das Dach in dem warmen Klima einen idealen Ort für festliche Abendessen, Filmvorführungen oder weitere Kunstaktionen dar.

Ce projet consiste en la rénovation et l'extension d'un lieu d'expositions d'art contemporain à partir d'un théâtre du début du XXe siècle et d'un grand magasin des années 1950. Selon l'architecte : « LTL a cherché à amplifier cette accumulation historique en transformant ce projet en une série d'additions tactiques intégrées. L'objectif principal était de créer un bâtiment qui stimule l'intérêt pour l'art contemporain, aussi bien dans les galeries qu'en ville. » L'un des gestes les plus visibles est d'accroître la « porosité » de l'immeuble en le perçant de blocs de verre feuilleté de couleur verte. Ces blocs saillants à l'extérieur éclairent l'intérieur. Là encore, la façade sur rue a été ouverte et vitrée pour améliorer l'éclairage. Plutôt que de transformer la galerie principale du second niveau en espace muséal traditionnel, les architectes ont préféré laisser très présents les murs en brique nue et les poutres métalliques de ce volume double-hauteur. Des parois d'accrochage coulissantes permettent de préserver le caractère brut de l'ancien bâtiment. Un escalier en bois monte du rez-de-chaussée vers le toit. Combinant un espace « vert » et le bois, cette toiture devient, sous ce climat chaud, un lieu idéal pour des dîners, des projections de films et diverses expositions que l'on peut apercevoir des immeubles environnants.

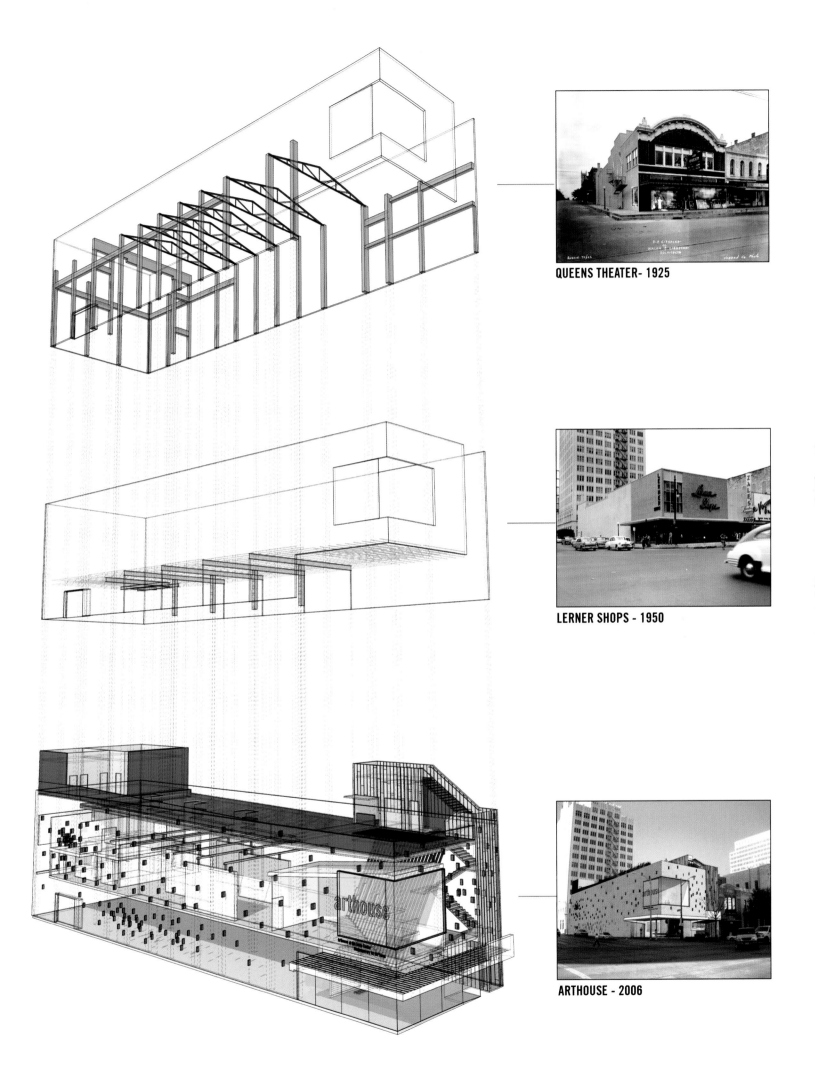

QUEENS THEATER- 1925

LERNER SHOPS - 1950

ARTHOUSE - 2006

A very basic rectangular floor plan and largely closed façades lead the architects to view their work as integrating "a series of tactical additions" to the building. Below, a perspective section shows the space of the entry lobby, gallery, and rooftop.

Ein sehr elementarer Grundriss und überwiegend geschlossene Fassaden lassen die Architekten ihre Arbeit als Integration »einer Reihe taktischer Erweiterungen« des Gebäudes verstehen. Der perspektivische Schnitt unten zeigt Eingangslobby, Galerie und Dachgarten.

Un plan très basique et des façades en grande partie aveugles ont amené les architectes à considérer leur intervention comme « une série d'addition tactiques ». En dessous, la coupe en perspective montre l'espace du hall d'entrée, la galerie et la terrasse en toiture.

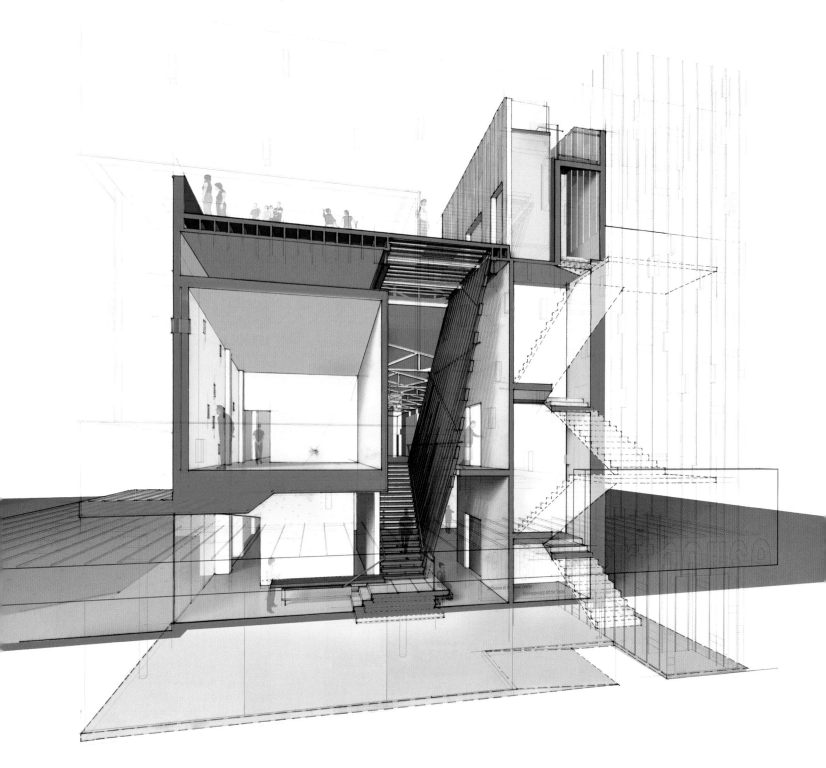

Above, a perspective drawing of the completed façade and, below, two views of the entrance sequence with its large staircase. The open glazed design of the lobby allows potential visitors to have a glimpse at the otherwise closed interior.

Oben eine perspektivische Zeichnung der fertigen Fassade, unten zwei Ansichten des Eingangsbereichs mit einem großen Treppenaufgang. Die Gestaltung der Lobby als offener, verglaster Raum erlaubt Besuchern einen Blick in das ansonsten geschlossene Innere.

Ci-dessus, perspective de la façade entière et, ci-dessous, deux vues de l'entrée et du grand escalier. Conçu comme un espace vitré ouvert, le hall permet aux visiteurs potentiels de jeter un coup d'œil dans ce bâtiment par ailleurs très fermé.

# 10

# RICHARD MEIER

RICHARD MEIER & PARTNERS
ARCHITECTS LLP
475 Tenth Avenue
New York, New York 10018
Tel: +1 212 967 6060
Fax: +1 212 967 3207
e-mail: mail@richardmeier.com

1001 Gayley Avenue
Los Angeles, California 90024
Tel: +1 310 208 6464
Fax: +1 310 824 2294
e-mail: mail@rmpla.com
Web: www.richardmeier.com

**RICHARD MEIER** was born in Newark, New Jersey, in 1934. He received his architectural training at Cornell University, and worked in the office of Marcel Breuer (1961–63) before establishing his own practice in 1963. In 1984, he became the youngest winner of the Pritzker Prize, and he received the 1989 RIBA Gold Medal. His notable buildings include The Atheneum, New Harmony, Indiana (1975–79); the Museum of Decorative Arts Frankfurt (1979–85); the High Museum of Art, Atlanta, Georgia (1980–83); the Canal Plus Headquarters Paris (1988–92); the City Hall and Library, The Hague (1986–1995); the Barcelona Museum of Contemporary Art, Barcelona (1987–95); and the Getty Center, Los Angeles, California (1984–97). Recent work includes the U.S. Courthouse and Federal Building, Phoenix, Arizona (1994–2000); the Jubilee Church, Rome (1996–2003); the Crystal Cathedral International Center for Possibility Thinking, Garden Grove, California (1998–2003); the Yale University History of Art and Arts Library, New Haven, Connecticut (2001–); and the 66 restaurant in New York. Present work includes the Beach House, a 12-story glass-enclosed condominium located on Collins Avenue in Miami (2004–07); the ECM City Tower, Pankrac City, Prague, Czech Republic (2004–07); 165 Charles Street (2003–06), a 16-story residential building located in Manhattan near the architect's Perry Street apartments (1999–2002); the Arp Museum, Rolandseck, Germany (1978–2007); and the Ara Pacis Museum, Rome (1995–2006).

# SAN JOSE CITY HALL
## SAN JOSE, CA
## 1998 - 2005

FLOOR AREA: 50 168 m² (540 000 ft.²)
CLIENT: The City of San Jose, Department of Public Works
PRINCIPALS IN CHARGE: Richard Meier, Michael Palladino, James R. Crawford
COST: $192 million

Part of a seven-block redevelopment area in downtown San Jose, the new City Hall is to be accompanied by a future theater and concert hall. The large complex includes an 18-story tower and two lower structures intended to house city departments and meeting rooms. Ample light and ventilation are provided with an emphasis on energy-efficient sustainable systems. The main entrance to the complex brings visitors through this plaza. Up to 2000 persons can gather in the outdoor area. The partially glazed and louvered entrance rotunda rises eight stories, and a ceremonial staircase rises from there to the second-floor city council chambers. Richard Meier has of course had ample experience in this kind of municipal facility, for example in The Hague (The Netherlands, 1986–95). The tower rises behind the dome and is "subtly layered and orchestrated to create an elaborately sun-screened low relief." While making reference to typical themes in civic architecture (the dome), the architects succeed in creating a bright modernity that has nothing to do with the heavy symbolism of the past, as is indeed appropriate for this California community.

Als Teil eines sieben Karrees umfassenden Sanierungsgebiets im Zentrum von San Jose wird die neue City Hall künftig von einem Theater und einer Konzerthalle ergänzt werden. Zu der weitläufigen Anlage gehören ein 18-geschossiges Hochhaus sowie zwei niedrigere Bauten, in denen städtische Ämter und Sitzungszimmer untergebracht werden sollen. Viel Licht und Luft gewährleisten Energie sparende, nachhaltige Systeme. Eine begrünte Zone auf der öffentlichen Platzanlage erinnert an die Bedeutung der Landwirtschaft für die heimische Ökonomie. Über diesen Platz erreichen Besucher den Haupteingang zu dem Komplex. Bis zu 2000 Personen können sich auf dem Freigelände versammeln. Die teilweise verglaste, mit Luftschlitzen versehene Eingangsrotunde erhebt sich über acht Geschosse, und ein repräsentativer Treppenaufgang führt von dort in die Geschäfts-

räume des Stadtrats im zweiten Stock. Richard Meier verfügt über reiche Erfahrung mit dem Bau solcher kommunaler Einrichtungen, beispielsweise in Den Haag (1986–94). Das sich hinter der Kuppel erhebende Hochhaus ist »subtil geschichtet und gegliedert, um ein sorgfältig vor Sonne geschütztes Flachrelief zu ergeben.« Zwar nimmt Meier Bezug auf typische Motive städtischer Architektur (die Kuppel), aber es gelingt ihm, eine dieser kalifonischen Stadt gemäße helle, freundliche Modernität zu schaffen, die nichts zu tun hat mit dem schweren Symbolismus der Vergangenheit.

Élément d'un programme de rénovation urbaine portant sur sept blocs du centre de San Jose, ce nouveau Centre municipal devrait être ultérieurement être complété par un théâtre et une salle de concert. Ce vaste complexe comprend une tour de 18 niveaux et deux constructions plus basses destinées aux bureaux et salles de réunion de l'administration municipale. Un éclairage et une ventilation naturels abondants participent à un dispositif de réduction de la consommation d'énergie. Un bosquet paysagé sur le parvis rappelle l'importance de l'agriculture pour l'économie locale. Cette place, qui peut accueillir jusqu'à 2000 personnes est située devant l'entrée principale. De la rotonde de l'entrée qui s'élève sur huit niveaux en partie vitrés et abrités par des persiennes part un grand escalier qui conduit aux salles de réunion du conseil municipal. Richard Meier possède une grande expérience de ce type d'équipement municipal avec, par exemple, l'hôtel de ville de La Haye (Pays-Bas, 1986–94). La tour qui s'élève derrière la coupole est « subtilement étagée et orchestrée pour créer un bas-relief élaboré de brise-soleil ». Tout en faisant référence à des thèmes typiques de l'architecture officielle, dont la coupole, Meier, réussit à apporter une modernité brillante sans rapport avec les lourds symboles du passé, solution sans doute appropriée pour une commune de Californie.

Richard Meier's mastery of the use of geometric grids to develop the spatial complexity and richness visible in these images appears to have attained new heights. Shelter from the sun is combined with a high degree of transparency and lightness.

Richard Meiers Meisterschaft im Umgang mit geometrischen Rastern zur Entfaltung räumlicher Komplexität und Vielfalt, die in diesen Bildern zu sehen ist, hat anscheinend eine neue Qualität erreicht. Schutz vor der Sonne geht einher mit einem hohen Maß an Transparenz und Leichtigkeit.

La maîtrise de Richard Meier dans l'utilisation des trames géométriques qui développent une complexité et une richesse spatiales étonnantes semble atteindre ici de nouveaux sommets. La protection contre le soleil se combine avec un degré élevé de transparence et de légèreté.

The main entrance to the complex is on East Santa Clara Street through a public plaza. The most arresting feature of this space is an eight-story semi transparent domed entrance hall intended as a venue for large public events.

Der Hauptzugang zu dem Gebäude an der East Santa Clara Street führt über eine öffentliche Platzanlage. Das reizvollste Attribut ist die überkuppelte achtgeschossige, halbtransparente Halle, die als Schauplatz großer öffentlicher Veranstaltungen vorgesehen ist.

L'entrée principale du complexe se fait par East Santa Clara Street sur une place publique. La caractéristique la plus frappante de cet espace est un hall d'entrée sous coupole semi-transparente de huit niveaux de hauteur qui peut accueillir de grandes manifestations.

The obvious coherence of the exterior forms of the City Hall and its open and spacious interior is a tribute to the architect's mastery of the rapport between light and space. Generous, bright volumes give municipal functions the dignity denied to them in much modern civic architecture.

Die augenfällige Übereinstimmung der äußeren Formgebung der City Hall und ihres offenen, weitläufigen Inneren ist dem meisterlichen Umgang des Architekten mit dem harmonischen Verhältnis von Licht und Raum zu verdanken. Großzügige, helle Baukörper geben kommunalen Aufgaben den würdevollen Rahmen, der ihnen von vielen modernen Behördenbauten verweigert wird.

La cohérence évidente entre les formes extérieures de cet hôtel de ville et son intérieur spacieux et ouvert est à porter au crédit de la maîtrise par Meier des rapports entre la lumière et l'espace. Les volumes généreux et brillamment éclairés confèrent aux fonctions municipales une dignité que trop de réalisations modernes leur dénient.

Within the breath taking rotunda, a ceremonial staircase leads visitors to the second floor of the City Hall, where the council chambers are located. The simplicity of the plan allows for the introduction of a good number of surprises, due in part to the layering of surfaces and types of cladding.

Von der eindrucksvollen Rotunde gelangen Besucher über eine repräsentative Treppe ins zweite Geschoss des Rathauses, wo sich die Geschäftsräume des Stadtrats befinden. Die Einfachheit des Grundrisses gestattet eine Reihe von überraschenden Motiven, teilweise dank der geschichteten Oberflächen und verschiedenartigen Verkleidungen.

Sous l'immense coupole aux dimensions à couper le souffle, l'escalier principal conduit les visiteurs à l'étage de la mairie abritant les salles de réunion du conseil. La simplicité du plan permet d'introduire un certain nombre de surprises architecturales grâce en partie à la stratification des surfaces et des types de revêtements.

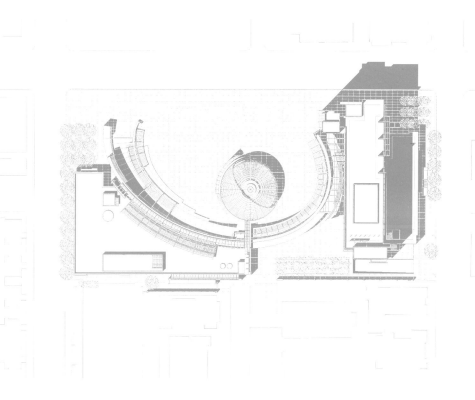

# SOUTHERN FLORIDA HOUSE
## PALM BEACH, FL
## 2004-07

FLOOR AREA: 957 m² (10 300 ft.²)
including garage and pool house
CLIENT: not disclosed
COST: not disclosed

Located on a lakefront site on the main boulevard in Palm Beach, this house has been designed for a client who is interested in art and has three small children. The architect stresses the relationship of the architecture to the landscape. As his description of the house reads, "The solid and stepping vertical planes at the entrance court seamlessly unite house and landscape. The entry ramp, the raised platform of the main floor, and the floating roof direct and frame the flow of space throughout the program. The floor and walls of the house extend beyond its structure, traversing the landscape and connecting the house with the sculpture garden, playground, swimming pool, and pool house." Although a dedication to "light, space and spirit" would seem to be a common denominator of most if not all of Richard Meier's architecture, these were the guiding words behind the design in this instance. Floor-to-ceiling windows offer lake views on three sides. Two staggered volumes contain on the one hand a double-height living room, dining room, kitchen, and upper level master bedroom and on the other hand a family room and library on the ground level with children's bedrooms above. Glass, steel, limestone, metal panel, and plaster are the main materials, with Richard Meier's trademark white dominating the color scheme.

Das Haus, das auf einem Seegrundstück am Hauptboulevard von Palm Beach steht, wurde für einen an Kunst interessierten Bauherrn mit drei kleinen Kindern entworfen. Der Architekt unterstreicht die Beziehung der Architektur zur Landschaft. In seiner Beschreibung des Hauses heißt es: »Die massiven, abgestuften vertikalen Flächen im Eingangshof bilden eine nahtlose Verbindung zwischen Haus und Landschaft. Die Eingangsrampe, die erhöhte Ebene des Hauptgeschosses sowie das schwebende Dach regeln das Fließen des Raums im gesamten Projekt. Boden und Wände des Hauses reichen über die Konstruktion hinaus, durchqueren die Landschaft und verbinden das Haus mit Skulpturengarten, Spielplatz, Schwimmbecken und Schwimmhalle.« Das Engagement für »Licht, Raum und

Geist« kann als gemeinsamer Nenner eines Großteils, wenn nicht des gesamten Œuvres von Richard Meier gelten, und auch diesem Entwurf lagen diese Leitbegriffe zugrunde. Auf drei Seiten bieten deckenhohe Fenster Ausblicke auf den See. In zwei versetzt angeordneten Baukörpern sind zum einen ein Wohnraum mit doppelter Geschosshöhe, Esszimmer, Küche und darüber das Elternschlafzimmer untergebracht, zum anderen ein Mehrzweckraum und die Bibliothek im Parterre und darüber die Kinderzimmer. Glas, Stahl, Kalkstein, Metallpaneele und Putz sind die Hauptmaterialien; die Farbskala wird von dem für Richard Meier typischen Weiß beherrscht.

Implantée en front de lac sur le boulevard principal de Palm Beach, cette maison a été conçue pour un client amateur d'art et ses trois enfants. L'architecte a mis l'accent sur la relation entre l'architecture et le paysage : « Les plans aveugles en gradins de la cour d'entrée font délicatement le lien entre la maison et le paysage. La rampe de l'entrée, le socle surélevé du niveau principal et le toit en suspension orientent et cadrent le flux de l'espace à travers le volume. Les sols et les murs de la maison se développent au delà de la structure, s'avancent dans le paysage et relient la maison au jardin de sculptures, au terrain de jeux, à la piscine et à son pavillon. » Bien que l'invocation à « la lumière, l'espace et l'esprit » semble un dénominateur commun à la plupart des réalisations de Richard Meier, si non à toutes, ces principes sont particulièrement bien illustrés par ce projet. Des fenêtres toute hauteur offrent des vues sur le lac sur trois côtés. Deux volumes en retrait contiennent d'une part un volume double hauteur regroupant séjour, salle-à-manger, cuisine et chambre principale à l'étage et d'autre part, une pièce pour la famille et une bibliothèque au rez-de-chaussée et les chambres d'enfants au-dessus. Le verre, l'acier, une pierre calcaire, des panneaux métalliques et le plâtre sont les principaux matériaux utilisés, la couleur dominante restant le blanc, signature de Richard Meier.

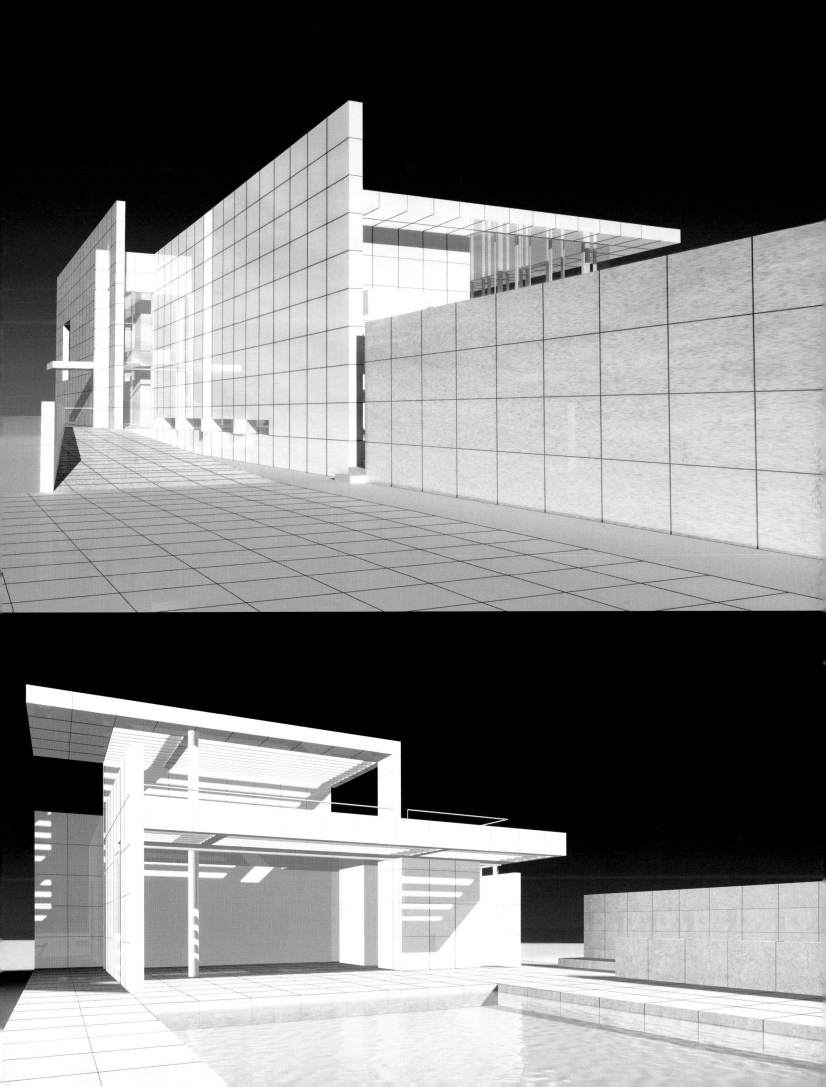

Turkish white limestone, and painted aluminum panels form the basic cladding materials for the house, which features one relatively closed façade and one more open side.

Zur Verkleidung des Hauses wurden in der Hauptsache weißer Kalkstein aus der Türkei sowie gestrichene Aluminiumplatten verwendet. Der Bau weist eine eher geschlossene Fassade und eine offenere Seite auf.

Du calcaire blanc de Turquie et des panneaux d'aluminium peints constituent les principaux matériaux de revêtement de cette maison qui possède une façade relativement fermée et une autre beaucoup plus ouverte.

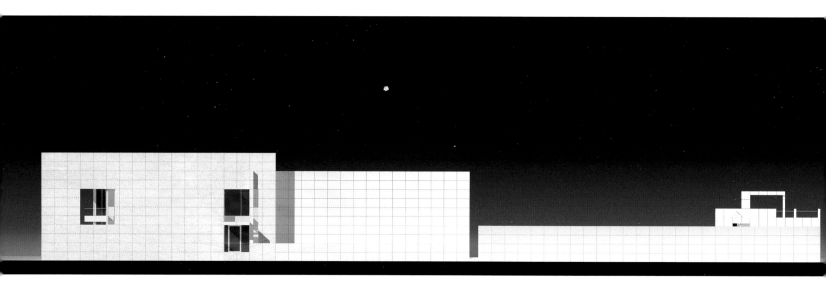

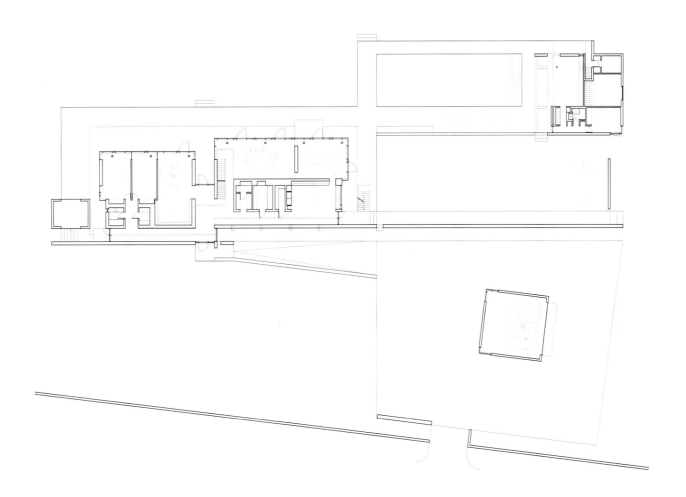

An orchestration of strictly geometric elements results in the kind of play of light and space that the architect is well known for. In this instance, a close rapport with the client has led to a particularly successful mixture of power and discretion.

Die Inszenierung streng geometrischer Elemente hat jenes Spiel von Licht und Raum zur Folge, für das der Architekt berühmt ist. Hier führte ein gutes Einverständnis mit dem Bauherren zu einer besonders gelungenen Mischung von Autorität und Besonnenheit.

L'orchestration d'éléments strictement géométriques aboutit à ce jeu entre lumière et volumes qui a fait la réputation de l'architecte. Ici, une collaboration étroite avec le client a conduit à un mélange particulièrement réussi de puissance et de discrétion.

# MORPHOSIS

**MORPHOSIS**
2041 Colorado Avenue
Santa Monica, California 90404

Tel: +1 310 453 2247
Fax: +1 310 829 3270
e-mail: studio@morphosis.net
Web: www.morphosis.net

Morphosis principal **THOM MAYNE**, born in Connecticut in 1944, received his Bachelor of Architecture degree in 1968 at USC, and his Master of Architecture degree at Harvard in 1978. He founded Morphosis in 1979 with Michael Rotondi, who left to create his own firm, RoTo. He has taught at UCLA, Harvard, Yale, the Berlage Institute, the Netherlands, the Barlett School of Architecture, London, and the Southern California Institute of Architecture (SCI-Arch), of which he was a founding Board Member. Some of the main buildings of Morphosis are the Lawrence House (1981); the Kate Mantilini Restaurant, Beverly Hills (1986); the Cedar's Sinai Comprehensive Cancer Care Center, Beverly Hills (1988); the Crawford Residence, Montecito (1987–90); as well as the Blades Residence, Santa Barbara, California (1992-97) and the International Elementary School, Long Beach, California (1997–99). Recent work includes the Hypo Alpe-Adria Center, Klagenfurt, Austria (2002), and Caltrans District 7 Headquarters, Los Angeles (2004). Current work includes the San Francisco Federal Building; the University of Cincinnati Student Recreation Center; the NOAA Satellite Operation Facility in Suitland, Maryland, featured here; Cooper Union's new academic building; the Wayne L. Morse U.S. Courthouse, Eugene, Oregon and social housing, Madrid. Thom Mayne was the winner of the 2005 Pritzker Prize.

# UNIVERSITY OF CINCINNATI CAMPUS RECREATION CENTER
## CINCINNATI, OH 2003 - 06

FLOOR AREA: 10 219 m² (110 000 ft.²) PROJECT SIZE: 32 516 m² (350 000 ft.²)
CLIENT: University of Cincinnati COST: $74 million
PRINCIPAL: Thom Mayne PROJECT MANAGER: Kim Groves
PROJECT ARCHITECT: Kristina Loock PROJECT DESIGNER: Ben Damron
DESIGN ARCHITECT: Morphosis / Executive: KZF Design

Faced with the task of creating a "multi-use recreational complex, including a food court, classrooms, student housing, a convenience store and varsity gymnasium facilities," the architects have chosen to "weave" the new architecture into the existing University of Cincinnati campus. Their problem had to do not only with buildings but with the landscape, which has become an integral part of their scheme and, as they say, "resolves many of the site's awkward idiosyncrasies, and the new cohesive texture embraces the complexities of campus life." Morphosis emphasizes campus circulatioin and movement through the new complex in describing the intervention, "Conceiving the main circulation corridor as a series of weaving strands, we placed "Main Street," the primary campus thoroughfare, in such a way as to concentrate and direct the movement of students. The contoured element of the new housing building funnels students onto the campus green, feeding the force-field of movement through a "pinch point." Secondary pedestrian paths penetrate, intertwine, and wrap buildings, further relaxing a reading of discrete objects on a homogeneous field, and substituting a thick mat of cohesive trajectories in its place."

Angesichts der Aufgabe, ein »Mehrzweck-Freizeitzentrum mit Gastronomie, Unterrichtsräumen, Studentenwohnungen, einem Einkaufsladen und Sportstätten« zu planen, entschieden sich die Architekten dafür, die neue Architektur in den vorhandenen Campus »einzubinden«. Die Schwierigkeiten hingen nicht nur mit den Gebäuden zusammen, sondern auch mit der Landschaft, die zu einem integralen Teil der Planung wurde. Den Architekten zufolge »löst sie viele der schwer zu handhabenden Merkmale des Geländes, und die neue zusammenhängende Struktur entspricht dem vielschichtigen Leben auf dem Campus«. Morphosis unterstreicht Wegeführung und Fortbewegung durch den neuen Komplex: »Wir konzipierten den Hauptschließungskorridor als Abfolge sich schlängelnder Linien und ließen ›Main Street‹, die Hauptstraße des Campus, so verlaufen, dass sie die Bewegung der Studenten zusammenfasst und steuert. Das profilierte Element des neuen Wohnheims lenkt die Studenten auf die Grünfläche des Campus und schickt den ständigen Strom der Passanten durch einen ›Engpass‹. Untergeordnete Fußwege führen durch Gebäude, verflechten sich in ihnen, umrunden sie, erleichtern so das Erfassen einzelner Objekte auf einem homogenen Feld und ersetzen ein dichtes Geflecht geschlossener Bewegungsabläufe.«

Confrontés à la tâche de créer « un complexe polyvalent, comprenant des restaurants en libre-service autour d'une cour, des salles de classe, des logements pour étudiants, un magasin de dépannage et divers équipements de gymnase, » les architectes ont choisi de « tisser » cette nouvelle architecture dans la trame existante du campus de l'université de Cincinnati. La difficulté tenait non seulement aux bâtiments existants mais au paysage devenu partie intégrante du projet qui, selon les architectes, « gomme de nombreuses caractéristiques maladroites du site, tout en prenant en compte la complexité de la vie du campus ». Morphosis a mis l'accent sur la circulation et le mouvement à travers le nouveau complexe : « En concevant le principal couloir de circulation comme une série de fils tissés, nous avons implanté « Main Street », le principal axe de circulation du campus, de façon à concentrer et orienter les mouvements des étudiants. La forme incurvée du nouvel immeuble de logements conduit les étudiants vers les pelouses du campus, concentrant le champ de forces du mouvement vers un « pincement ». Des cheminements piétonniers secondaires pénètrent les bâtiments, les enveloppent et les relient, ce qui facilite la lecture d'objets discrets posés dans un champ homogène, et ils remplacent un épais tapis de trajectoires cohésives. »

"We were interested," say the architects," in developing a series of connective events to engage peripheral flows on the campus in order to generate or augment an urban density and to encourage, rather than dampen, the polyvalent nature of social experience on campus."

»Wir waren daran interessiert«, sagen die Architekten, »eine Reihe verbindender Elemente zu entwickeln, um die peripheren Passantenströme auf dem Campus zu bündeln; damit wollten wir urbane Verdichtung schaffen und den vielschichtigen Charakter sozialer Erfahrungen auf dem Campus fördern anstatt ihn zu hemmen.«

« Ce qui nous intéressait, c'était de développer une série d'événements connectifs qui suscitent des flux périphériques afin de générer ou d'accroître la densité urbaine et d'encourager, plutôt que de réfréner, la nature polyvalente des échanges sur le campus », ont précisé les architectes.

Tom Vac chairs by Ron Arad seem to fit into the cafeteria space in an effortless way. The swimming pool is rendered dynamic and exciting by the sharp cut out forms of the roof and glazed areas.

Die Tom-Vac-Stühle von Ron Arad fügen sich harmonisch in den Raum der Cafeteria ein. Die Schwimmhalle wirkt dank der scharf ausgeschnittenen Dachformen und verglasten Bereiche dynamisch und anregend.

Les fauteuils « Tom Vae » de Ron Arad paraissent s'adapter sans effort à l'espace de la cafétéria. La piscine est dynamisée et donc rendue plus intéressante par les puissantes découpes de la toiture et des zones vitrées.

# NOAA SATELLITE OPERATION CONTROL FACILITY SUITLAND, MD 2003-06

FLOOR AREA: 19 324 m² (208 000 ft.²) SITE AREA: 80 825 m² (870 000 ft.²)
CLIENT: General Services Administration COST: $54 million
PRINCIPAL, MORPHOSIS: Thom Mayne PROJECT MANAGER: Paul Gonzales
PROJECT ARCHITECT: David Rindlaub PROJECT DESIGNER: Jean Oei
JOINT VENTURE: Morphosis / Einhorn Yaffee Prescott

In describing this project, the architects quote from Rachel Carson's work *The Sense of Wonder* (1956), "Those who dwell, as scientists or laymen, among the beauties and mysteries of the earth are never alone or weary of life." NOAA, the National Oceanic & Atmospheric Administration, is known to many Americans through their satellite imagery (www.noaa.gov), which permits live coverage of hurricanes, for example. The program of Morphosis for this project was to create a "satellite operation control center including office space, computer rooms, satellite control rooms, conference center, exercise facility, café with 24 hr.–7 day operational capability." The architects have chosen to make the "eyes and ears" of NOAA, a field of antennas used to communicate with 16 satellites, very visible on top of the three-story building. As they explain, "The iconic antennas comprise the dominant visual register of the project. The departments that operate as 'the brain' of the operation—mission control, launch control, and computer processing—are housed in the slender bar." Below this bar, the architects have placed what they call the "body", a partially submerged, disc-shaped building that contains double-height space for offices and support services. Given the environmental mission of NOAA, it was logical too for the architects to develop a design scheme that "prioritizes open space, reduces the presence of built form, and integrates architecture with landscape."

Wenn sie dieses Projekt beschreiben, zitieren die Architekten aus Rachel Carsons Werk *The Sense of Wonder* (1956): »Jene, die als Wissenschaftler oder Laien inmitten der Schönheiten und Geheimnisse der Erde leben, sind niemals allein oder des Lebens überdrüssig.« NOAA, die National Oceanic & Atmospheric Administration, ist vielen Amerikanern durch ihr Satellitenbildprogamm (www.noaa.gov) bekannt, das beispielsweise die Livesendung von Hurrikans gestattet. Morphosis gestaltete für dieses Projekt »ein Kontrollzentrum für Satelliteneinsätze mit Büros, Computerräumen, Satellitenkontrollräumen, Konferenzzentrum, Sporteinrichtungen sowie ein Café, das rund um die Uhr betrieben werden soll.« Die Architekten entschieden sich dafür, die »Augen und Ohren« von NOAA, ein Antennenfeld für die Kommunikation mit 16 Satelliten, sehr augenfällig auf dem Dach des dreigeschossigen Gebäudes zu platzieren. Sie führen dazu

aus: »Die symbolträchtigen Antennen stellen die beherrschende visuelle Ebene des Projekts dar. Die als ›Gehirn‹ der Anlage fungierenden Abteilungen, Kommandoüberwachung, Startüberwachung und Computerbearbeitung, sind in einem schlanken Riegel untergebracht.« Unter diesem Riegel hat der von den Architekten so genannte Körper, ein z. T. versenkter, scheibenförmiger Bauteil, Platz gefunden, in dem doppelgeschossige Räume für Büros und Versorgungsdienste untergebracht sind. Angesichts der umweltrelevanten Mission der NOAA erschien es den Architekten darüber hinaus folgerichtig, eine Entwurfsplanung zu entwickeln, die »dem offenen Raum Vorrang gibt, die Präsenz gebauter Form mindert und die Architektur in die Landschaft einbindet«.

Dans leur descriptif, les architectes citent l'œuvre de Rachel Carson *The Sense of Wonder* (1956): « Ceux, savants ou profanes, qui demeurent parmi les beautés et les mystères de la terre ne sont jamais seuls ni lassés de la vie. » NOAA, la National Oceanic & Atmospheric Administration, est connue de beaucoup d'Américains par ses images prises par satellite (www.noaa.gov) qui permettent, par exemple, de suivre la progression des ouragans. Le programme confié à Morphosis consistait en la création « d'un centre de contrôle des opérations satellitaires comprenant des bureaux, des salles d'ordinateurs, des salles de contrôle des satellites, un centre de conférence, des installations de gymnastique, un café, le tout fonctionnant 7 j/7, 24 h/24. » Morphosis a choisi de rendre les « yeux et les oreilles » de NOAA, ses antennes de communication avec les 16 satellites, très visibles au sommet de cet immeuble sur trois niveaux: « La valeur iconique de ces antennes fournit le registre visuel dominant du projet. Les départements qui sont le « cerveau » des opérations, du contrôle des missions, des lancements, du traitement informatique sont logés dans la barre. » Sous celle-ci a été placé ce que les architectes appellent "le corps", un bâtiment en forme de disque qui contient des volumes double hauteur pour les bureaux et les services techniques. Dans l'esprit de la mission environnementale de NOAA, il était également logique de développer un projet qui« donne la priorité aux espaces à plan ouvert, réduise la présence du bâti et intègre l'architecture dans le paysage ».

The emphasis placed by the architects on the formidable array of satellite dish antennas required for the NOAA facility give it a kind of science-fiction quality that is accentuated by the cantilevered and suspended supports.

Das Gewicht, das die Architekten der für das Kontrollzentrum der NOAA erforderlichen Phalanx von Parabolantennen zumessen, verleiht der Anlage einen Science-Fiction-Charakter, der von den auskragenden, eingehängten Stützen noch verstärkt wird.

L'accent mis par les architectes sur ce formidable déploiement de paraboles et d'antennes donne à l'immeuble de la NOAA un petit air de science-fiction qu'accentuent les supports en porte-à-faux ou en suspension.

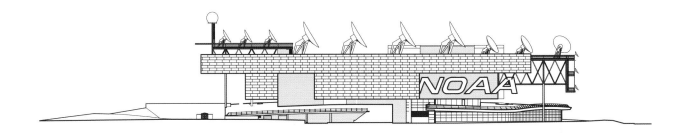

If the relation to satellites is a determining factor for the exterior appearance of the NOAA building, its interior is all about the business of analyzing the constant flow of data provided through the antennas.

Während die Verbindung zu Satelliten der entscheidende Faktor für die äußere Erscheinung des NOAA-Gebäudes ist, wird das Innere gänzlich von der Analyse des dank der Antennen beständig eingehenden Datenstroms bestimmt.

Si les relations satellitaires constituent le facteur déterminant de l'aspect extérieur de l'immeuble, l'intérieur favorise la concentration requise pour l'analyse des flux constants de données captés par les antennes.

# 12

# ERIC OWEN MOSS

**ERIC OWEN MOSS ARCHITECTS**
8557 Higuera Street
Culver City, California 90232

Tel: +1 310 839 1199
Fax: +1 310 839 7922
e-mail: mail@ericowenmoss.com
Web: www.ericowenmoss.com

Born in Los Angeles, California, in 1943, **ERIC OWEN MOSS** received his Bachelor of Arts degree from UCLA in 1965, and his Master of Architecture from UC Berkeley in 1968. He also received a Master of Architecture degree from Harvard in 1972. He opened his own firm, located in Culver City, California, in 1973. He has been a Professor of Design at the Southern California Institute of Architecture (SCI-Arc) since 1974, and has been director of the school since 2003. His built work includes the Central Housing Office, University of California, Irvine, Irvine, California (1986–89); the Lindblade Tower, Culver City (1987–89); the Paramount Laundry, Culver City (1987–89); the Gary Group, Culver City (1988–90); The Box, Culver City (1990–94); the I.R.S. Building, Culver City (1993–94); and the Samitaur Complex, Culver City (1994–96). Recent built work includes the Stealth; the Umbrella; and the Beehive, all in Culver City, California. Recent projects include Queens Museum of Art, Queens, New York (2001–03); a proposal for the Mariinsky Cultural Center, St. Petersburg (2001–03); New Holland, St. Petersburg (2001–03); the Jose Vasconcelos Library of Mexico, Mexico City (2003–04); the Conjunctive Points Theater Complex; the Gateway Art Tower; and a parking garage and offices (the Pterodactyl), located in Culver City.

# THE BEEHIVE
## CULVER CITY, CA
## 2000 - 01

FLOOR AREA: 919 m² (9890 ft.²)
CLIENT: Frederick and Laurie Samitaur Smith
COST: not disclosed

Located at 8520 National Boulevard near a number of Eric Owen Moss's other projects, this is an office building. As Moss says, "The Beehive isn't a form. It's forms. And the forms change." A new two-story structure was built in the footprint of a dilapidated warehouse surrounded on three sides by existing buildings. The architect was thus almost obliged to concentrate the design effort on a 10.7-meter (35-ft.) façade. The architect explains that "The skin of the building is a shingle system of glass planes and thin sheet metal walls that is expressed on both the interior and exterior." A reception area on the ground floor reveals stairs that rise to the second floor, from which a second stairway leads visitors to the roof terrace. Four bent interior columns define the exterior wall and respond to the requirements of the interior space. Here, as in many other projects in Culver City, Eric Owen Moss has carried forward his career-long campaign to change a forlorn warehouse area into usable, attractive space.

Dieses Bürogebäude liegt am National Boulevard 8520 in der Nähe einer Reihe anderer Projekte von Eric Owen Moss. Moss sagt dazu: »Der Bienenkorb [beehive] ist keine Form. Es sind Formen. Und die Formen verändern sich.« Auf dem Fundament eines verwahrlosten Lagerhauses entstand ein zweigeschossiger Bau, der auf drei Seiten von vorhandenen Gebäuden umgeben ist. Folglich blieb dem Architekten kaum eine andere Wahl, als seine Gestaltungsbemühungen auf die 10,7 m lange Fassade zu konzentrieren. Er erläutert, dass »die Außenhaut des Gebäudes aus einem System schindelartig angeordneter Glasflächen und dünner Metallwände besteht, das im Innen- wie Außenraum sichtbar ist«. Von einem Empfangsbereich im Parterre führt eine Treppe zur zweiten Ebene, von wo Besucher über eine weitere Treppe auf die Dachterrasse gelangen. Vier schräg stehende Pfeiler im Inneren bestimmen die Außenwand und entsprechen der Gliederung im Innenraum. Wie mit zahlreichen anderen Projekten in Culver City hat Eric Owen Moss auch mit diesem Gebäude das Projekt fortgeführt, an dem er seit Beginn seiner Laufbahn arbeitet: ein verlassenes Areal mit Lagerhäusern in ein wieder nutzbares, ansehnliches Viertel zu verwandeln.

Cet immeuble de bureaux situé 8520 National Boulevard se trouve à proximité de plusieurs autres réalisations d'Eric Owen Moss. Pour celui-ci : « La ruche [beehive, en anglais] n'est pas une forme. Mais des formes. Et les formes changent. » Ce nouveau bâtiment de deux étages a été construit à la place d'un entrepôt délabré entouré sur trois côtés de bâtiments existants, ce qui a obligé l'architecte à se concentrer sur la façade de 10,7 m de large : « La peau de l'immeuble est un système de bardeaux de panneaux de verre et de fines plaques métalliques, identique à l'intérieur et à l'extérieur. » De la zone de réception du rez-de-chaussée part un escalier vers le second niveau, d'où un autre escalier mène à la terrasse sur le toit. Quatre colonnes internes incurvées définissent le mur extérieur. Comme avec plusieurs de ses autres projets pour Culver City, Eric Owen Moss poursuit sa campagne de transformation d'une friche industrielle en un quartier actif et séduisant.

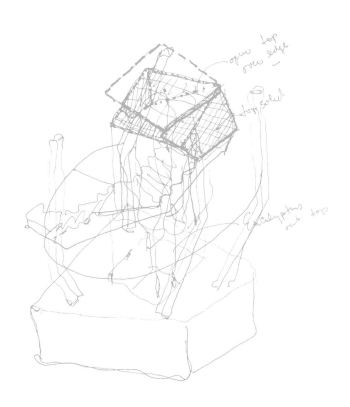

"The skin of the building is a shingle system of glass planes and thin sheet metal walls that is expressed on both the interior and exterior." The sense of forms that have been cut out and reinstated in a more sculptural and dynamic form is even stronger here than in other Culver City buildings by the architect.

»Die Außenhaut des Gebäudes besteht aus einem System schindelartig angeordneter Glasflächen und dünner Metallwände, das im Innen- wie Außenraum sichtbar ist«. Der Eindruck von Formen, die ausgeschnitten und in plastischerer und dynamischerer Form wieder eingesetzt wurden, tritt hier noch deutlicher hervor als bei anderen Gebäuden des Architekten in Culver City.

« La peau du bâtiment est un système de bardeaux en panneaux de verres et de murs minces en tôle métallique qui s'exprime aussi bien à l'extérieur qu'à l'intérieur. » Le sentiment d'être devant des formes découpées et remises en place selon une disposition plus sculpturale et dynamique est encore plus forte que dans d'autres réalisations de l'architecte à Culver City.

Although the name of the building gives the impression that it is rather directly inspired by the natural form of the beehive, in reality, it responds to the internal and external requirements of the site and the program.

Obgleich der Name des Gebäudes den Eindruck vermittelt, es sei unmittelbar von der natürlichen Form des Bienenkorbs angeregt, reagiert es in Wahrheit auf die inneren und äußeren Bedingungen des Baugeländes und der Ausschreibung.

La forme de ruche, qui se retrouve dans le nom du bâtiment, répond en réalité aux contraintes internes et externes du terrain et du programme.

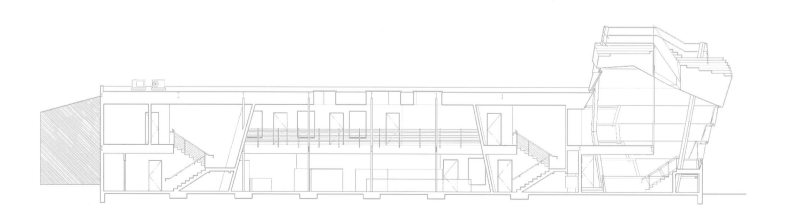

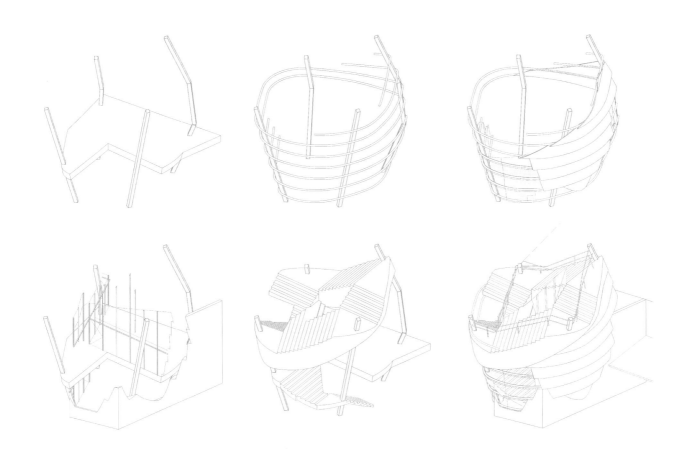

# 13

# POLSHEK PARTNERSHIP

**POLSHEK PARTNERSHIP ARCHITECTS, LLP**
320 West 13th Street
New York, New York 10014

Tel: +1 212 807 7171
Fax: +1 212 807 5917
e-mail: info@polshek.com
Web: www.polshek.com

The Clinton Presidential Center was a collaboration between Richard Olcott and James S. Polshek. **RICHARD OLCOTT** has been a member of the firm since 1979. He received a Bachelor of Architecture degree from Cornell University in 1979. Olcott is the recipient of the 2003–04 Founders Rome Prize Fellowship awarded by the American Academy in Rome. Among Olcott's current designs are the WGBH Public Broadcasting Station Headquarters, Brighton, Massachusetts and the renovation and expansion of the Yale University Art Gallery, New Haven, Connecticut. Recent projects include the Seamen's Church Institute, New York, New York (1991); the New York Times Printing Plant, Queens, New York (1997); the Iris and B. Gerald Cantor Center for Visual Arts at Stanford University, California (1998); the Oklahoma City Civic Center Music Hall, Oklahoma City, Oklahoma (2001); the Judy and Arthur Zankel Hall at Carnegie Hall, New York, New York (2003); and the Holland Performing Arts Center, Omaha, Nebraska (2005). Since 1996, Richard Olcott has been a Commissioner on the New York City Landmarks Preservation Commission. Born in Akron, Ohio, in 1930, **JAMES POLSHEK** is the founding partner of Polshek Partnership Architects. He received a Master of Architecture degree from Yale University in 1955, and established his practice in New York in 1963. Among Polshek's current projects are the Vietnam Veteran's Memorial Education Center and the Newseum/Freedom Forum Foundation World Headquarters, Washington, District of Columbia. His recent buildings include the Santa Fe Opera Theater, Santa Fe, New Mexico (1998); the Rose Center for Earth and Space at the American Museum of Natural History, New York, New York (2000); the Scandinavia House, New York, New York (2001); and the Peter Norton Symphony Space, New York, New York (2002). James Polshek is a long-time educator and served from 1972 to 1987 as dean of the Columbia University Graduate School of Architecture, Planning, and Preservation.

# WILLIAM J. CLINTON PRESIDENTIAL CENTER

## LITTLE ROCK, AR
## 2001 - 04

FLOOR AREA: Bridge Building: 7432 m² (80 000 ft.²);  Archive Building: 6503 m² (70 000 ft.²)
CLIENT: William J. Clinton Foundation COST: not disclosed
ARCHITECT: Polshek Partnership Architects LLP  DESIGN PARTNERS: Richard M. Olcott, James S.Polshek
PARTNER-IN-CHARGE: Joseph L. Fleischer PROJECT MANAGERS: Kevin P. McClurkan, Molly McGowan
PROJECT DESIGNER: Kate Mann ASSOCIATE ARCHITECTS: Polk Stanley Rowland Curzon Porter Architects, Ltd.;
Witsell Evans Rasco Architects and Planners: Woods Carradine Architects

Located in a new 11-hectare (27-acre) public park located on the south bank of the Arkansas River directly east of the city of Little Rock, the new William J. Clinton Presidential Center represents a clear break with earlier institutions of the same nature. Although presidential libraries have become something of a tradition in the United States, this is the first effort to achieve a high level of architectural quality, while meeting the programmatic requirements of a library, archive, and visitor center. The site of a trading post created by the French explorer Bernard de la Harpe in 1722, Little Rock is the capital of Arkansas and has a population of approximately 190 000 people. James Stuart Polshek conceived of the Center itself as an airborne form that stands raised off the ground so that the park can flow beneath it. The actual form makes reference of the Six Bridges of Little Rock and is also, according to the architect, "a metaphor for the progressive goals of the Clinton administration." The main exhibition space has natural light. While metal and glass dominate the raised volume, the Archive Building is an "earthbound" stone and concrete structure. The site of the Center, a former warehouse area at the edge of the city, included two historic structures, the Rock Island Railway Bridge and the 1226 m² 1899 Choctaw Station, which has been renovated and integrated into the complex.

Das östlich der Stadt Little Rock in einem neu angelegten, 11 ha großen, öffentlichen Park am Südufer des Arkansas River liegende William J. Clinton Presidential Center stellt einen klaren Bruch mit früheren Institutionen dieser Art dar. Obgleich ehemaligen Präsidenten zugeeignete Bibliotheken in den Vereinigten Staaten inzwischen zur Tradition geworden sind, hat man sich hier zum ersten Mal um überdurchschnittliche Architektur bemüht; gleichzeitig wollte man den programmatischen Erfordernissen von Bibliothek, Archiv und Besucherzentrum gerecht werden. Ursprung von Little Rock, der Hauptstadt des Bundesstaates Arkansas, ist eine von dem französischen Entdecker Bernard de la Harpe im Jahr 1722 begründete Handelsniederlassung; heute zählt Little Rock etwa 190 000 Einwoh-ner. James Stuart Polshek entwarf das eigentliche Center als eine quasi über dem Boden schwebende Form, unter der sich der Park ausbreiten kann. Der Bau nimmt Bezug auf die sechs Brücken von Little Rock und stellt, den Architekten zufolge, darüber hinaus »eine Metapher für die fortschrittlichen Ziele der Regierung Clinton« dar. Der Hauptausstellungsraum wird von Tageslicht erhellt. Während der erhöht stehende Baukörper in erster Linie aus Metall und Glas besteht, hat man für das Archivgebäude auf »erdgebundenere« Materialien wie Stein und Beton zurückgegriffen. Auf dem am Rand der Innenstadt gelegenen, vormals für Lagerhäuser genutzten Baugelände, gibt es zwei historische Bauwerke, die Rock Island Railway Bridge sowie die 1226 m² große Choctaw Station von 1899, die renoviert und in den Komplex integriert wurde.

Site d'un comptoir commercial fondé par l'explorateur français Bernard de la Harpe en 1722, Little Rock (190 000 habitants) est la capitale de l'Arkansas. Implanté dans un nouveau parc public de 11 hectares sur la rive sud de l'Arkansas River dans la partie est de la ville, le William J. Clinton Presidential Center constitue une franche rupture au sein de ce type d'architecture. Bien que les bibliothèques présidentielles soient devenues une sorte de tradition aux États-Unis, il s'agit là d'une première tentative pour atteindre à un haut niveau de qualité architecturale, tout en répondant aux exigences programmatiques d'une bibliothèque, d'un centre d'archives et d'un centre d'accueil pour visiteurs. James Stuart Polshek a conçu ce centre comme une forme suspendue au-dessus d'un parc, faisant ainsi référence aux « Six ponts » de Little Rock et, selon l'architecte, « à une métaphore des objectifs progressistes de l'administration Clinton ». Le principal espace d'exposition, en éclairage naturel. Si le verre et le métal sont prépondérants dans le volume surélevé, le bâtiment des archives est en pierre et en béton. Le site du centre, d'anciens entrepôts aux limites de la ville, englobe deux bâtiments historiques, le pont de chemin de fer de Rock Island et la gare de Chocstaw de 1226 m² datant de 1899 rénovée et intégrée au complexe.

With its central super structure and long cantilevered projection, the building recalls the shape of an aircraft carrier in section, even if exterior photos somewhat temper that vision.

Mit ihrem zentralen Oberbau und der langen Auskragung erinnert die Form des Gebäudes an die Schnittdarstellung eines Flugzeugträgers, selbst wenn die Außenansichten diesen Eindruck etwas mindern.

Par sa superstructure centrale et ses longues projections en porte-à-faux, le bâtiment rappelle en coupe la forme d'un porte-avion, même si les photos atténuent quelque peu cette vision.

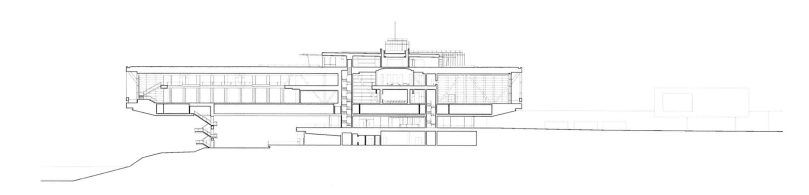

The computer perspective above corresponds closely to the final result, seen in the photograph below. The success of the project is also related to its integration into a new riverside park, rich in local history.

Die Computerperspektive oben entspricht weitgehend dem gebauten Endergebnis. Der Erfolg des Projekts hängt auch mit seiner Einbindung in einen neu entstandenen, geschichtsträchtigen Park am Fluss zusammen.

La perspective ci-dessus correspond de très près à la réalisation finale (photo ci-dessous). La réussite du projet est par ailleurs liée à son intégration dans un nouveau parc en bordure de rivière, site chargé d'histoire.

American rhetoric notwithstanding, it is rare that presidential libraries in any way reflect the ideals of democracy and transparency so often invoked during political campaigns. The Clinton Library is an exception to that rule, offering a bright, modern vision.

Ungeachtet amerikanischer Rhetorik geschieht es höchst selten, dass die Gedächtnisbibliotheken der Präsidenten in irgendeiner Weise die während der Wahlkämpfe so häufig beschworenen Ideale von Demokratie und Transparenz widerspiegeln. Clintons Bibliothek stellt mit ihrer hellen, modernen Architektur in dieser Hinsicht eine Ausnahme dar.

Rhétorique américaine mise à part, il est rare qu'une bibliothèque présidentielle reflète en quoi que ce soit les idéaux de démocratie et de transparence si souvent invoqués dans les campagnes électorales. La bibliothèque Clinton illustre une vision moderne et éclairée de ce type de bâtiment et fait exception à cette règle.

A sense of openness is maintained wherever possible, here in the 73-meter-long (240-foot-long) and 12-meter-high (30-foot-high) space that gives the general public an overview of the Clinton years. In the plans below, the archive building is seen to the right.

Wo immer möglich, wird in diesem 73 m langen, 12 m hohen Raum, in dem Besucher einen Überblick über Clintons Regierungszeit erhalten, der Eindruck der Offenheit bewahrt. Der Grundriss rechts unten ist der des Archivgebäudes.

Le sentiment d'ouverture est maintenu partout où c'est possible, par exemple ici dans cet espace de 73 m de long et 12 m de haut qui donne au grand public un panorama des années Clinton. Dans les plans ci-dessous, le bâtiment des archives figure à droite.

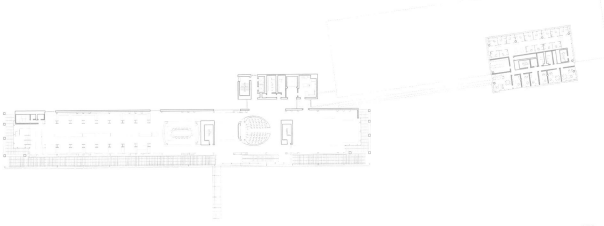

# #14

# ANTOINE PREDOCK

ANTOINE PREDOCK ARCHITECT PC
300 12th Street NW
Albuquerque, New Mexico 87102

Tel: +1 505 843 7390
Fax: +1 505 243 6254
e-mail: studio@predock.com
Web: www.predock.com

Born in 1936 in Lebanon, Missouri, **ANTOINE PREDOCK** studied at the University of New Mexico and received his Bachelor of Architecture degree from Columbia University in 1962. He has been the principal of Antoine Predock Architect PC since 1967. He was a visiting lecturer at the Southern California Institute (SCI-Arc) from 1995 to 2000 and has held several other teaching positions. His notable buildings include the Nelson Fine Arts Center, Arizona State University, Tempe, Arizona (1990); the Zuber House, Phoenix, Arizona (1989), the Hotel Santa Fe, Euro Disney, Marne-la-Vallée, France (1992); the Classroom/Laboratory/Administration Building, California Polytechnic State University, Pomona, California (1993); the American Heritage Center and Art Museum, University of Wyoming, Laramie, Wyoming (1993); the Civic Arts Plaza, Thousand Oaks Performing Arts Center and City Hall, Thousand Oaks, California (1994); the Ventana Vista Elementary School, Tucson, Arizona (1994); Arizona Science Center, Phoenix, Arizona (1996); Gateway Center, University of Minnesota, Minneapolis, Minnesota (2000). Recent work includes the Tacoma Art Museum, Tacoma, Washington (2003); the Flint River Quarium, Albany, Georgia (2004); the Austin City Hall and Public Plaza, Austin, Texas (2004); the Student Activity and Recreation Center, Ohio State University, Columbus, Ohio (2006). Current work includes the Science Canyon, Academy School, Colorado Springs, Colorado (2008); the Doudna Fine Arts Center, Eastern Illinois University, Charleston, Illinois (2007); the U.S. Federal Courthouse, Las Cruces, New Mexico (2008); the National Palace Museum, Chiayi County, Taiwan (2008); and the Canadian Museum for Human Rights, Winnipeg, Manitoba (2008). In 2006, Antoine Predock received the AIA Gold Medal.

# AUSTIN CITY HALL AND PUBLIC PLAZA
## AUSTIN, TX
## 2001 - 04

FLOOR AREA: 10 962 m² (118 000 ft.²)
CLIENT: City of Austin, Texas, Economic Growth + Redevelopment Services
COST: $50 million EXECUTIVE ARCHITECT: Cotera + Reed Architects

This new facility is located at the edge of the Warehouse district and on the shores of Town Lake. Predock has sought to create a transition between the grid of restaurants, nightlife, offices, and housing in the area and the natural setting beyond. As he says, "Terraces slide out of the building into the plaza in an analogous relationship to geologic forces in the hill country surrounding Austin that produces the limestone overhangs known as balcones. These terraces are shaded with trees and become habitable, prime locations for viewing the activities on the plaza and Town Lake beyond." The complex contains several city departments, together with the offices of the mayor, city manager, the City Council Chambers, and offices as well as a café and gallery. A large limestone wall emerges from the bedrock on the site and leads to the two-story limestone base of the building. Copper is used as a skin material and for the folded roof. The sharply angled, cantilevered upper volumes of the structure give it a decidedly dynamic appearance. A four-story open lobby with bridges at each level brings light into the building. Water emerges from an indoor "canyon,", runs through a group of limestone boulders, and down toward the lake. An outdoor amphitheater, protected from the sun by "a trellised structure made up of photovoltaic cells," allows the building to send surplus electricity to the local power grid.

Das neue Gebäude steht am Rand des Warehouse Districts, einem ausgedehnten Vergnügungsviertel, sowie am Ufer des Town Lake. Predock war bestrebt, einen Übergang von den Restaurants, Nachtklubs, Büros und Wohnhäusern in der Gegend zur natürlichen Landschaft zu schaffen. Wie er dazu ausführt »schieben sich Terrassen aus dem Gebäude in die Plaza hinein, entsprechend den geologischen Kräften, die in der hügeligen Umgebung wirken und die als ›balcones‹ bekannten Kalksteinüberhänge entstehen lassen. Diese Terrassen mit ihren schattigen Bäumen werden zu angenehmen, beliebten Orten, von denen aus man das Treiben auf der Plaza und darüber hinaus den Town Lake überschauen kann « In dem Komplex sind mehrere städtische Ämter untergebracht, zusammen mit den Büros des Bürgermeisters und des City Managers, den Amtszimmern des Stadtrats und weiteren Büros sowie einem Café und Galerien. Eine große Kalksteinwand er

hebt sich aus dem felsigen Untergrund des Geländes und führt zu dem zwei Geschosshöhen umfassenden Kalksteinsockel des Gebäudes. Zur Verkleidung der Außenhaut und für das Faltwerkdach wurde Kupfer verwendet. Die scharfwinkligen, vorkragenden oberen Elemente des Baus verleihen ihm ein entschieden dynamisches Aussehen. Eine vier Geschosse umfassende, offene Lobby mit Brücken auf jeder Ebene lässt Licht in das Gebäude einfallen. Aus einer »Schlucht« im Gebäudeinneren steigt Wasser auf, läuft durch eine Gruppe von Kalksteinblöcken und weiter hinunter zum See. Im Freien befindet sich außerdem ein Amphitheater, das durch eine »gitterartige Konstruktion mit Fotovoltaikzellen« Schatten erhält; diese erzeugen einen Energieüberschuss, der in das örtliche Netz eingespeist werden kann.

Ce nouveau bâtiment municipal se trouve en limite du quartier des entrepôts sur la rive du Town Lake. Predock a cherché à créer une transition entre la trame d'un ensemble de restaurants, clubs de nuit, immeubles de bureaux et d'habitation et le cadre naturel : « Les terrasses glissent du bâtiment vers la place dans une relation analogue a celle des forces géologiques du paysage de collines entourant Austin qui a produit ces surplombs de calcaire appelées *balcones*. Ombragées d'arbres, elles sont devenues un lieu idéal pour observer l'animation de la place et du lac. » Le complexe abrite plusieurs services municipaux ainsi que les bureaux du maire, et du responsable de gestion municipale, des salles du conseil municipal et des bureaux ainsi qu'un café et une galerie d'exposition. Un grand mur en calcaire qui s'élève du sol rocheux conduit au socle en pierre, haut de deux niveaux, de l'immeuble. La façade et le toit à grands plis sont recouverts de cuivre. Les volumes supérieurs inclinés en porte-à-faux créent une apparence résolument dynamique. Un hall de quatre niveaux de haut doté de passerelles à chaque étage éclaire l'intérieur du bâtiment. L'eau qui court dans un « canyon » intérieur s'écoule entre des blocs de calcaire jusqu'au lac. Un amphithéâtre de plein air, protégé du soleil par une « structure en treillis à cellules photovoltaïques » permet a l'immeuble de produire un surplus d'électricité qui est réintroduit dans le réseau local

In contrast with the office blocks that stand behind it in the image below (left), the Austin City Hall gives the impression that its massive slabs arise from the earth itself, the result more of geological activity than any modernist tower.

Im Gegensatz zu den benachbarten Bürobauten (unten links), vermittelt das Rathaus von Austin den Eindruck, als stiegen seine wuchtigen Platten direkt aus der Erde auf, als seien sie eher die Folge geologischer Aktivität als der Entwurf eines Architekten.

Par contraste avec les tours de bureaux qui se dressent derrière lui sur la photo ci-dessous (à gauche), le Centre municipal d'Austin donne l'impression que ses dalles massives ont surgi du sol dans un esprit plus « géologique » que celui des tours modernistes voisines.

The densely designed project makes space for all required factilities, such as the auditorium pictured below. Openings are sometimes of unexpected form and materials tend to emphasize the rooting of the building in the land of the site.

Das kompakt konzipierte Projekt bietet sämtlichen geforderten Einrichtungen, so dem unten abgebildeten Auditorium, Raum. Hier und da überraschen die Öffnungen mit neuartigen Formen, und die Materialien tragen zur Verankerung des Gebäudes an seinem Standort bei.

Ce projet dense réussit à contenir tous les éléments du programme, comme l'auditorium reproduit ci-dessous. Les ouvertures ont parfois des formes inattendues et le choix des matériaux tend à mettre en valeur l'enracinement du bâtiment dans le sol.

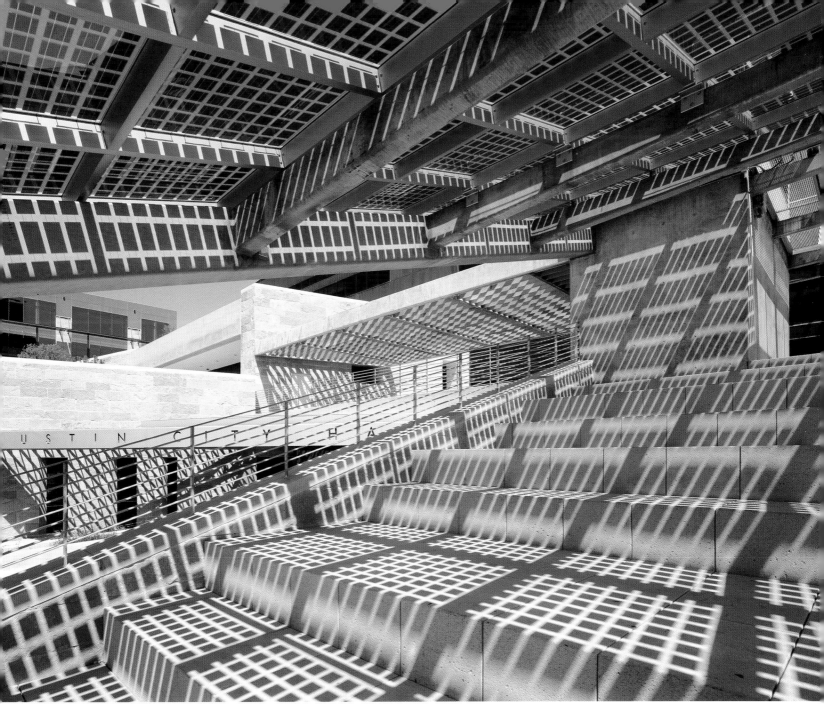

The sense that the structure rises up from the earth is retained inside as well as out. A heavy layering of materials contributes to the impression of solidity conveyed by the architecture.

Das Empfinden, der Bau erhebe sich aus der Erde, wird im Inneren ebenso bewahrt wie beim Außenbau. Zu diesem von der Architektur vermittelten Eindruck trägt eine dicke Schichtung von Materialien bei.

Ce sentiment que la structure est née du sol même s'éprouve aussi bien à l'intérieur qu'à l'extérieur. La stratification très présente des matériaux contribue à l'impression de massivité donnée par cette architecture.

# 15

# RURAL STUDIO

**RURAL STUDIO**
College of Architecture, Design, and
Construction
School of Architecture
202 Dudley Commons
Auburn University, Alabama 36849

Tel: + 1 334 844 5426
Fax: + 1 334 844 5458
e-mail: rstudio@auburn.edu
Web: www.ruralstudio.com

**SAMUEL MOCKBEE,** born in 1945, founded Mockbee/Coker Architects, based in Canton, Mississippi, and in Memphis, Tennessee, with Coleman Coker in 1978. The firm completed a number of structures, including the Barton House and the Cook House, both located in Mississippi. They have had a considerable reputation in the region established through their contemporary interpretations of local architecture. Samuel Mockbee taught at Yale, at the University of Oklahoma, and was a Professor of Architecture at Auburn University beginning in 1991. He created the Rural Studio with Dennis K. Ruth in 1993 to improve living conditions in rural Alabama and to include hands-on experience in architectural pedagogy, while "extending the study of architecture into a socially responsible context." Three programs, lasting from a semester to a year, are organized for students at Auburn. Mockbee seems to have inspired the Rural Studio to use the vocabulary of simple materials and regional inspiration for which Mockbee/Coker is known. He died at the end of 2001, but it was immediately decided that the work of the Rural Studio would go on. The studio is today under the direction of Bruce Lindsey, School of Architecture Head, and Professor Andrew Freear. **ANDREW FREEAR** was born in Yorkshire, England. He graduated from the Polytechnic of Central London and the Architectural Association (AA) in London. He taught at the University of Illinois before joining Auburn University. Recently completed community projects are the Akron Senior Center, Hale County, Alabama (2001-02); the Lee County AIDS Alabama House, Alabama (2002-03); and the Perry Lakes Pedestrian Bridge, Marion, Alabama (2003-04). Recently completed houses include the Lucy House in Mason's Bend and the Shiles House, both completed in Hale County, Alabama (2001-02); and the Music Man House, Hale County, Alabama (2002-03).

# 100-FOOT BIRDING TOWER
# PERRY LAKES PARK
# MARION, AL
# 2004-06

HEIGHT: 30.5 meters (100 ft.)
COST: not disclosed
DESIGNED BY: Natalie Butts, Coley Mulcahy,
Paul Howard, Adrienne Brady

Designed as a thesis project at Auburn University by Natalie Butts, Coley Mulcahy, Paul Howard, and Adrienne Brady, the 100-Foot Birding Tower is located in Perry Lakes Park in central Alabama. The four students located an 80-year-old fire tower in Sumter County, Alabama, which they were given for $25 on condition that they move it themselves to the new site in Marion. They took down the tower over a period of 15 days and transported the pieces, weighing 8165 kilos (18 000 pounds), to Birmingham, where they had parts regalvinized and brought to the Park. They used helical foundations and no concrete due to site accessibility limitations. A 91-meter-long (100-yard-long) boardwalk designed by the students leads from the nearby Ridge Trail to the tower. The structure stands above the tree level, allowing bird watchers to observe approximately 200 local species. Although this project may not qualify in the usual sense as one of the most remarkable new structures in the United States in recent years, it does demonstrate an entirely different approach to building than that of by most established architects. This is a starting point for young students, and an auspicious one at that.

Das von Natalie Butts, Coley Mulcahy, Paul Howard und Adrienne Brady für ihre Abschlussarbeit an der Auburn University entworfene Projekt befindet sich im Perry Lakes Park in Alabama. Die vier Studenten machten einen 80 Jahre alten Feuerturm in Sumter County, Alabama, ausfindig, der ihnen für 25 Dollar überlassen wurde unter der Bedingung, dass sie ihn selbst an seinen neuen Standort in Marion transportieren würden. In 15 Tagen zerlegten sie den Turm in Einzelteile und schafften die insgesamt 8165 kg wiegenden Bestandteile nach Birmingham, wo sie neu verzinkt und anschließend in den Perry Lakes Park transportiert wurden. Aufgrund der eingeschränkten Zugänglichkeit des Standorts verwendeten sie für die Gründung Spiralarmierung und keinen Beton. Ein von den Studenten konzipierter, 91 m langer Bohlengang führt vom in der Nähe verlaufenden Ridge Trail zum Turm. Das Bauwerk erhebt sich über die Wipfel der Bäume und ermöglicht es Vogelenthusiasten, etwa 200 einheimische Arten zu beobachten. Obgleich dieses Projekt im herkömmlichen Sinn nicht als einer der bemerkenswertesten Neubauten jüngerer Zeit in den Vereinigten Staaten gelten kann, veranschaulicht es doch eine gänzlich andere Auffassung vom Bauen als die der meisten etablierten Architekten. Für Architekturstudenten können Projekte dieser Art ein vielversprechendes Sprungbrett in die Zukunft sein.

Projet de thèse de Natalie Butts, Coley Mulcahy, Paul Howard et Adrienne Brady à Auburn University, cette « tour aux oiseaux » de 30 m de haut se dresse dans le Perry Lakes Park, au cœur de l'Alabama. Ces quatre étudiants avaient remarqué une tour de pompiers vieille de quatre-vingts ans dans le comté de Sumter qui leur fut donnée pour 25 dollars à condition qu'ils la déplacent eux-mêmes vers le nouveau site. Ils la démontèrent en 15 jours et transportèrent les 8 tonnes de métal à Birmingham pour faire regalvaniser certains éléments avant de les transporter dans le parc. L'accessibilité au site étant limitée, ils ont fait appel à des fondations sans béton. Une allée de planches de 91 m de long également dessinée par eux conduit de la Ridge Trail – un chemin – à la tour. La structure dépasse la cime des arbres et permet aux ornithologues amateurs d'observer quelque 200 espèces locales d'oiseaux. Si ce projet n'est pas la structure nouvelle élevée aux États-Unis la plus remarquable de ces dernières années, il illustre une approche entièrement différente du bâti de celle de beaucoup d'architectes confirmés. C'est un point de départ prometteur pour ces jeunes étudiants.

Despite the relatively rudimentary nature of its design, the Birding Tower, as it is inscribed in the natural setting, becomes an elegant work of architecture, proving that substantial means are not indispensible when seeking to accomplish a specific task with a limited budget.

Ungeachtet des eher unvollkommenen Charakters dieses Projekts wird der in seine natürliche Umgebung geschickt eingefügte Birding Tower zu einem eleganten Bauwerk, mit dem der Nachweis erbracht wird, dass sich eine spezifische Aufgabe durchaus mit einem begrenzten Budget angemessen erfüllen lässt.

Malgré la nature relativement rudimentaire de ses plans, la « Tour aux oiseaux » bien inscrite dans son cadre naturel devient une élégante œuvre d'architecture, preuve qu'il est parfaitement possible d'atteindre un objectif précis dans le cadre d'un budget limité.

# 16

# SCOGIN ELAM

**MACK SCOGIN**
**MERRILL ELAM ARCHITECTS**
111 John Wesley Dobbs Avenue, NE
Atlanta, Georgia 30303

Tel: +1 404 525 6869
Fax: +1 404 525 7061
e-mail: office@msmearch.com
Web: www.msmearch.com

**MACK SCOGIN** was born in 1943 in Atlanta, Georgia. He graduated in architecture from the Georgia Institute of Technology in 1966. Since 1990, he has been an adjunct professor of architecture at the Harvard School of Design, where he was the Chairman of the Department of Architecture (1990–2000). Scogin also taught at the Georgia Institute of Technology (1987–89) and at Ohio State University (2003–04). Prior to founding Scogin Elam and Bray in 1984, which became Mack Scogin Merril Elam Architects in 2000, he was with Heery and Heery architects and engineers in Atlanta (1967–84), as President, Chief Operating Officer, and Director of Design. **MERRILL ELAM** was born in 1943 in Nashville, Tennessee. She received her Bachelor of Architecture degree at Georgia Institute of Technology (1971) and an MBA at Georgia State University (1982). She has taught at the Georgia Institute of Technology, Ohio State University, Harvard and Yale University, and held the Gehry International Visiting Chair in Architectural Design at the University of Toronto (2005). She was an architect and senior associate at Heery and Heery (1969–81). Notable work includes a satellite museum of the High Museum, Georgia-Pacific Center, Atlanta, Georgia (1986) and the reinstallation of the permanent collection of the High Museum of Arts, Atlanta (1997); the House Chmar, Atlanta, (1989); the law library of Arizona State University, Tempe, Arizona (1993); the Clark Atlanta University Art Gallery (1996); and the Mountain Tree House, Dillard, Georgia (2001). Recent work includes the Berkeley music library, California (2004); the Austin E. Knowlton School of Architecture at Ohio State University, Columbus, Ohio (2004); the Wang Campus Center and Davis Garage at Wellesley College, Massachusetts (2005); and the new Gates Center for computer sciences at Carnegie Mellon University, Pittsburgh, Pennsylvania (2005). Current works include the Zhongkai Sheshan Villas in Shanghai, China; a U.S. Federal Courthouse, Austin, Texas; and the Clemson Automotive Research Center, Greenville, South Carolina.

# LULU CHOW WANG CAMPUS CENTER

## WELLESLEY COLLEGE WELLESLEY, MA 2001-05

FLOOR AREA: 4645 m² (49 998 ft.²) campus center
plus 565 parking spaces and relocation of shops building
CLIENT: Wellesley College
COST: $65 million

Encompassing the greater part of the western half of the Wellesley College campus, the Wang Campus Center, Davis Garage, and related Alumnae Valley projects bring substantial changes to one of the more attractive colleges in the eastern United States. Located 21 kilometers (13 miles) west of Boston, Wellesley was founded in 1875 and aims to "provide an excellent liberal arts education for women who will make a difference in the world." Aside from the main campus center building, the project includes a 20 000 square foot building for the Campus Trade Shops, a 4000 square foot building for the campus police, the renovation and re-design of the campus chilled-water plant, and the redesign of the Campus Central Utility Plant environs. As the architects have explained, "Our strategy for designing the campus center includes the following. The building's relation to the land is affirming but complex. It accedes to historically established principles wherever possible. It emphasizes and dramatizes the natural topography. The building rejects transcendental paradigms. It embraces local and existing conditions as sources of richness and beauty. It celebrates the variety and roughness of topography. The building is a beacon. It is open and light."

Das Wang Campus Center, die Davis Garage und zugehörige Projekte des Alumnae Valley nehmen den Großteil der westlichen Hälfte des Campus von Wellesley College ein und erforderten erhebliche Veränderungen bei einem der schöneren Colleges im Osten der Vereinigten Staaten. Das 21 km westlich von Boston gelegene Wellesley wurde 1875 gegründet und ist bestrebt »Frauen, die das Zeug haben, etwas zu verändern, eine hervorragende geisteswissenschaftliche Ausbildung zu bieten«. Neben dem Hauptgebäude des Campuszentrums umfasst das Projekt ein 1850 m² großes Gebäude für Geschäfte, eine 370 m² große Wache für die Campuspolizei, die Renovierung und den Umbau der Kühlwasseranlage sowie die Umgestaltung des Umfelds der zentralen Versorgungsanlage. Wie die Architekten erklärten, »beinhaltet unsere Strategie bei der Durchbildung des Campuszentrums folgendes: Die Beziehung des Gebäudes zum Umland ist bestätigend, aber vielschichtig. Wo immer möglich, hält sie sich an historisch anerkannte Prinzipien. Sie unterstreicht und veranschaulicht die topografischen Gegebenheiten. Das Gebäude lehnt abstrakte Paradigmen ab. Es bezieht lokale, existierende Bedingungen als Quellen von Vielfalt und Schönheit ein. Es würdigt den Formenreichtum und die Rauheit der Topografie. Der Bau ist ein Leuchtturm. Er ist offen und hell.«

À 13 km de Boston, le Wellesley College a été fondé en 1875 pour « offrir une excellente éducation dans le domaine des arts libéraux aux femmes qui sauront faire la différence dans le monde. » Recouvrant la plus grande partie de la moitié ouest du campus de Wellesley, le Wang Campus Center, le Davis Garage et les projets pour la « Vallée des anciens » ont apporté des changements substantiels à l'un des établissements les plus dynamiques de cette partie de l'Est des États-Unis. En dehors de l'immeuble principal du campus, le projet englobe un bâtiment de 1 800 m² pour les boutiques du campus, un de 360 m² pour la police, la rénovation et le réaménagement de l'usine de réfrigération et le réaménagement des services techniques centraux. « Notre stratégie pour le Campus Center, expliquent les architectes s'appuie sur une relation entre l'immeuble et le terrain qui est à la fois affirmée mais complexe. Elle tient à des principes historiques établis, à chaque fois que c'est possible, et met spectaculairement en valeur la topographie. L'immeuble rejette les paradigmes transcendantaux. Il prend en compte les contraintes locales comme autant de sources de richesse et de beauté. Il célèbre la variété et la brutalité de la topographie. Ce bâtiment est un phare. Il est ouvert et léger. »

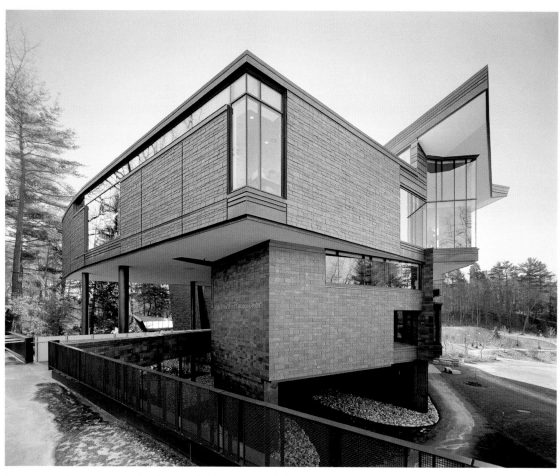

The dynamic angled and cantilevered forms of the new building contrast rather strongly with the rather bucolic atmosphere of the Wellesley campus, perhaps just the kind of energy required to keep students awake…

Die dynamisch abgewinkelten und vorkragenden Formen des neuen Gebäudes stehen in Kontrast zur eher bukolischen Atmosphäre des Campus von Wellesley – vielleicht eine Quelle der Energie für müde Studentinnen?

Les formes dynamiques en porte-à-faux du nouveau bâtiment contrastent assez fortement avec l'atmosphère plutôt bucolique du campus de Wellesley. Peut-être cet affichage d'énergie favorise-t-il l'éveil des étudiantes…

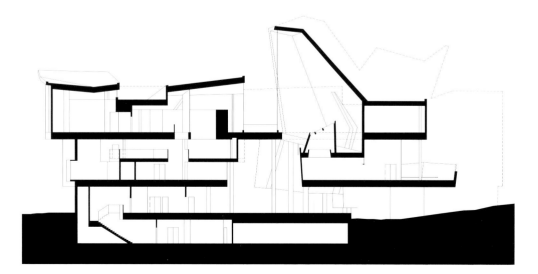

The architects started with the statement that "the buildings best loved within the Wellesley community have aesthetic properties which blend with those of the landscape." The layered complexity of these images does evoke a geological or topographic concern.

Die Architekten begannen mit der Erkenntnis, dass »das bei der Gemeinschaft von Wellesley beliebteste Gebäude sich durch ästhetische Eigenschaften auszeichnet, die mit denen der Landschaft verschmelzen«. Die geschichtete Komplexität dieser Bilder lässt den Gedanken an eine geologische oder topologische Beziehung aufkommen.

Les architectes sont partis du constat que « les bâtiments les plus aimés de Wellesley possèdent des caractéristiques esthétiques qui se fondent avec celles du paysage ». La stratification complexe que montre ces images rappelle la prise en compte de la réalité topographique ou géologique du site.

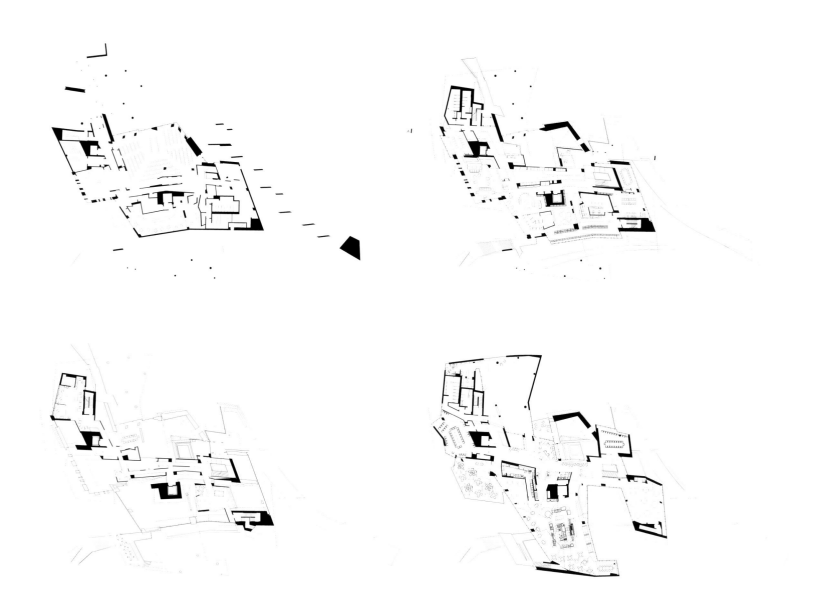

Above left, the terrace level plan, with a multi-purpose space, catering kitchen, pub, bistro, and café. Above right, the College Road level with a convenience store, post office, and a lobby/forum. Just above, left, the Mezzanine level with administrative offices, a meeting room, and a student lounge. Finally, just above right, the Upper level with a bookstore, main dining area, and terrace.

Oben links: Grundriss der Terrassenebene mit Mehrzweckraum, Partyküche, Pub, Bistro und Café. Oben rechts: Ebene der College Road mit Einkaufsladen, Post und Lobby/Forum. Unten links: Ebene des Zwischengeschosses mit Verwaltungsbüros, Versammlungsraum und Studentenlounge. Unten rechts: obere Ebene mit Buchhandlung, Hauptmensa und Terrasse.

En haut à gauche: plan du niveau de la terrasse avec espace polyvalent, cuisine, pub, bistrot et café. En haut à droite: au niveau de College Road, une boutique, une poste et un forum-hall d'accueil. En bas à gauche: niveau en mezzanine avec des bureaux administratifs, une salle de réunion et un salon pour étudiants. En bas à droite: le niveau supérieur abritant librairie, réfectoire principal et terrasse.

Lighting, both day and night, contributes to the powerful architecture, relating it, in the case of the large glazed areas seen to the right, to the natural setting and the rest of the campus.

Bei Tag und Nacht unterstreicht die Beleuchtung die ausdrucksstarke Architektur und verbindet sie, wie im Fall der rechts sichtbaren großen Glasflächen, mit der Landschaft und dem übrigen Campus.

De jour comme de nuit, l'éclairage contribue à la puissance de cette architecture qu'il rattache ainsi au cadre naturel et au reste du campus, comme dans le cas des vastes plans vitrés, à droite.

# 17

# WILLIAMS AND TSIEN

**TOD WILLIAMS**
**BILLIE TSIEN ARCHITECTS**
222 Central Park South
New York, New York 10019

Tel: +1 212 582 2385
Fax: +1 212 245 1984
e-mail: mail@twbta.com
Web: www.twbta.com

**TOD WILLIAMS** was born in Detroit, Michigan, in 1943. He received his Bachelor of Arts degree (1965), and Master of Fine Arts (1967) from Princeton. He began his own practice in New York in 1974. He taught at the Cooper Union as well as at Harvard, Yale, the University of Virginia, and Southern California Institute of Architecture (SCI-Arc). Tod Williams received a mid-career Prix de Rome in 1983. **BILLIE TSIEN** was born in Ithaca, New York, in 1949. She received her Bachelor of Arts degree from Yale, and her Master of Architecture from UCLA (1977). She has been a painter, and graphic designer (1971–75). She has taught at Harvard, City College in New York, and Yale. Their built work includes the Feinberg Hall, Princeton, New Jersey, (1986); Hereford College, University of Virginia, Charlottesville, Virginia (1992); as well as two renovations and extensions of the Phoenix Art Museum, Phoenix, Arizona (1996 and 2006). Additional projects include the Williams Natatorium, Cranbrook Academy, Bloomfield, Michigan (2001); the Johns Hopkins University Student Art Center, Baltimore, Maryland (2001); and the American Folk Art Museum, New York (2002), which was the winner of an 2003 AIA National Honor Award. Current projects include the Hong Kong Asia Society Headquarters (2008); the C.V. Starr East Asian Library at U.C. Berkeley, California (2008); and an information technology campus, Mumbai, India (2008).

# HOUSE ON EASTERN LONG ISLAND
## SHELTER ISLAND, NY
## 2001 - 03

FLOOR AREA: 464 m² (5000 ft.²)
CLIENT: not disclosed
COST: not disclosed
PROJECT ARCHITECTS: Paul Schulhof, Betty Chen

Located on a bluff overlooking the Atlantic Ocean, this house is on the side of Shelter Island that faces away from Sag Harbor. It is built on a cast-in-place concrete lower level and foundation. Brazilian granite panels (1.5 x 2.5 meter [5 x 8 foot] slabs) are used for the exterior cladding, while New York Bluestone floors and solid cherry walls were selected for the interior. Designed for a "physically active single man," the house was erected on the site of a previous residence that had burned down, leading the client to want architecture that would "engender a sense of permanence." An elevated courtyard frames an ocean view, and serves as an "outdoor room" connecting the volumes formed by the main house and the garage. A guest bedroom, kitchen, dining area, and living room are located on this level. The master bedroom is on the lower floor, together with two additional bedrooms. A game room is located beneath the garage and is connected to the house by a glass corridor. As the architects explain, "The interior furnishings are still spare because the owner spends most of his time involved in outdoor physical activity. However the house is a powerful shell: weighty, set into the ground like a large rock outcropping overlooking the sea and the sky."

Das Haus steht auf einem Steilufer über dem Atlantik, auf der Sag Harbor abgewandten Seite von Shelter Island. Es wurde auf einem Untergeschoss und Fundament aus Ortbeton errichtet. Die Außenseite ist mit brasilianischen Granítplatten (Größe 1,5 x 2,5 m) verkleidet, während im Inneren die Wahl auf Böden aus New Yorker Blausandstein und massive Kirschholzwände fiel. Das für einen »sportlich aktiven Junggesellen« entworfene Haus entstand an der Stelle eines früheren, durch Brand zerstörten Wohnhauses, was beim Auftraggeber den Wunsch nach einer Architektur mit »einem Gefühl von Dauerhaftigkeit« auslöste. Ein erhöhter Innenhof rahmt den Blick aufs Meer und dient als »Zimmer im Freien«, das die Baukörper des Haupthauses und der Garage verbindet. Auf dieser Ebene befinden sich ein Gästezimmer, Küche und Essbereich sowie das Wohnzimmer. Das Hauptschlafzimmer und zwei weitere Schlafräume finden sich auf der unteren Ebene. Ein Freizeitraum liegt unterhalb der Garage und ist mit dem Haus durch einen gläsernen Korridor verbunden. Den Architekten zufolge »ist das Haus nur spärlich möbliert, weil der Eigentümer die meiste Zeit mit sportlichen Aktivitäten im Freien verbringt. In jedem Fall ist das Haus ein machtvolles Gehäuse: in den Boden gesetzt wie ein großer Felsvorsprung mit Aussicht auf Meer und Himmel.«

En bordure d'une crête donnant sur l'océan Atlantique, cette maison se trouve sur Shelter Island face à Sag Harbor. Elle repose sur des fontations et un sous-sol en béton coulé sur place. Des dalles de 1,5 x 2,5 m en granit du Brésil ont été utilisées pour le parement des façades, la pierre « New York Bluestone » pour les sols, des panneaux en cerisier pour les murs intérieurs. Conçu pour « un célibataire ayant une activité physique importante » la maison a été érigée sur le site d'une ancienne résidence qui avait brûlé, ce qui avait conduit ce client à souhaiter une architecture qui « engendre un sens de permanence ». Une cour surélevée cadre une vue de l'océan et sert de « pièce d'extérieur » qui relie les volumes formés par la maison principale et le garage. La chambre d'amis, la cuisine et la zone de repas et le séjour sont situés à ce niveau. La suite principale se trouve au niveau inférieur ainsi que deux chambres supplémentaires. Une salle de jeux se trouve sous le garage, reliée à la maison par un couloir vitré. Comme l'explique l'architecte : « L'aménagement intérieur est encore minimal car le propriétaire consacre le plus clair de son temps à des activités sportives. Cependant la maison est une coque : pesante, posée sur le sol comme un gros affleurement de rocher donnant sur la mer et le ciel ».

Concrete structures, clad with 1.5 x 2.5 meter (5 x 8 foot) panels of blue Brazilian granite, the house, set on a bluff overlooking the Atlantic, assumes a certain solidity as seen from the water's edge.

Vom Ufer aus gesehen vermitteln die beiden, mit 1,5 x 2,5 m großen Platten aus blauem, brasilianischem Granit verkleideten Beton-bauten, die auf einem Steilufer über dem Atlantik stehen, Solidität.

Faite d'éléments en béton habillés de panneaux de 1,5 x 2,5 m en granit bleu du Brésil, la maison implantée sur un escarpe-ment surplombant l'Atlantique présente, vue de l'eau, une certaine massivité.

As seen in plans, below right, the house assumes a much less cubic or block-like form than its exterior appearance indicates. As in many of their projects, the architects work in great detail on the juxtaposition of materials and on the finishes.

Wie aus den Grundrissen rechts unten ersichtlich, hat das Haus eine weit weniger kubische oder blockartige Form, als sein äußeres Erscheinungsbild vermuten lässt. Wie bei vielen ihrer Projekte legten die Architekten großen Wert auf kontrastreiche Materialien und Oberflächen.

Les plans en bas à droite montrent que la forme de la maison est beaucoup moins cubique ou en « bloc » que son aspect extérieur ne le laisse supposer. Comme dans beaucoup de leurs projets, les architectes accordent le plus grand soin à la juxtaposition des matériaux et aux finitions.

The relative simplicity of the surfaces seems to blend all the more with the surface of the earth and the more distant ocean horizon in the image below.

Auf dem Bild unten scheint die relative Schlichtheit der Oberflächen mit der Erd-oberfläche und dem weiter entfernten Horizont des Meeres zu verschmelzen.

La simplicité relative du plan (ci-dessous) semble se fondre avec le sol et l'horizon plus lointain.

Window frames in the house are teak on the exterior and redwood on the interior. The floors are a honed bluestone and walls are either sandblasted concrete, natural plaster, or solid cherry panels. The furnishings are "spare because the owner spends most of his time in outdoor physical activity."

Die Fensterrahmen des Hauses sind außen aus Teakholz, innen aus Redwood gefertigt. Die Fußböden bestehen aus poliertem Blausandstein, die Wände entweder aus sandgestrahltem Beton, naturbelassenem Putz oder massiven Kirschbaumpaneelen. Die Möblierung ist »spärlich, weil der Eigentümer die meiste Zeit mit sportlichen Aktivitäten im Freien verbringt«.

Les encadrements de fenêtres sont en teck à l'extérieur et en bois de séquoia à l'intérieur. Les sols sont grès bleu poncé et les murs en béton sablé, plâtre naturel ou panneaux en cerisier massif. Le mobilier est « peu abondant parce que le propriétaire consacre la plupart de son temps à des activités physiques de plein air. »

The palette of materials used by the architects, coming together in sometimes unexpected combinations, is a hallmark of their
work, here moving readily from stone to
wood to glass, animating the interior space
and contrasting it with the sea view.

Die Auswahl der von den Architekten
verwendeten Materialien, die bisweilen in
unerwarteten Kombinationen aufeinander
treffen, ist typisch für ihre Arbeit; hier wechseln
sie von Stein über Holz zu Glas, beleben so
den Innenraum und kontrastieren ihn mit
dem Ausblick aufs Meer.

La palette des matériaux utilisés et leurs
mariages parfois inattendus est la marque du
travail des architectes. Ici les rapports entre
la pierre, le bois et le verre animent l'espace
intérieur et contrastent avec la vue sur
l'océan.

"The house," write the architects, "is a powerful shell: weighty, set into the ground like a large rock outcropping overlooking the sea and the sky."

»In jedem Fall ist das Haus«, so die Architekten, »ein machtvolles Gehäuse: in den Boden gesetzt wie ein großer Felsvorsprung mit Aussicht auf Meer und Himmel.«

« La maison, écrivent les architectes, est une coque pleine de force: pesante, posée sur le sol comme un gros affleurement de rocher donnant sur la mer et le ciel. »

# PHOTO CREDITS IMPRINT

CREDITS: PHOTOS/PLANS/DRAWINGS/CAD DOCUMENTS

18, 21, 23-25 © Asymptote: Hani Rashid and Lise Anne Couture / 26, 29-30 top, 31 bottom, 32-35 © Nic Lehoux / 30 bottom, 31 top © Bohlin Cywinski Jackson / 36, 39-40 top, 41 bottom, 43-44 top, 45 bottom, 46-47 © Sally Schoolmaster / 40 bottom, 41 top, 44 bottom, 45 top © Boora Architects / 48, 51-53, 55 bottom left, 56-57 © DSRNY / 55 top and bottom right © John Louie / 58, 61-64 top, 65 bottom © Roland Halbe / 64 bottom, 65 top © Gehry Partners / 66, 69, 70 bottom, 71, 72 bottom, 73-75 © Paul Warchol / 70 top, 72 top, 81-82 © Steven Holl Architects / 77-80, 83 © Andy Ryan / 84, 87-89 © Michael Jantzen / 90, 93, 94 top left and right, 95 bottom, 96 top, 97 © Erich Ansel Koyama / 94 bottom, 96 bottom © Jones, Partners: Architecture / 98, 101-113 top © Michael Moran / 103 bottom, 105-107 © Lewis.Tsurumaki.Lewis / 108, 111-117 top © Scott Frances/Esto / 117 bottom, 119-121 © Richard Meier & Partners Architects / 122, 125-131, 133-134 top, 135-137 © Roland Halbe / 134 bottom © Morphosis / 138, 141-142 top, 143, 144 top, 145 bottom © Tom Bonner / 142 bottom, 144 bottom, 145 top © Eric Owen Moss Architects / 146, 149-150 top, 151 bottom, 152 top, 153 top © Timothy Hursley / 150 bottom, 151 top, 152 bottom, 153 bottom © Polshek Partnership Architects / 154, 157, 158 bottom, 159-161 © Timothy Hursley / 158 top © Antoine Predock Architect / 162, 165-168, 171-174 top, 175, 177 © Timothy Hursley / 174 bottom, 176 © Mack Scogin Merrill Elam Architects / 178, 181-182 top and bottom, 183-185 top, 186-191 © Michael Moran / 182 center, 185 bottom © Tod Williams Billie Tsien Architects

To stay informed about upcoming TASCHEN titles, please request our magazine at www.taschen.com/magazine or write to TASCHEN, Hohenzollernring 53, D-50672 Cologne, Germany, contact@taschen.com, Fax: +49-221-254919. We will be happy to send you a free copy of our magazine which is filled with information about all of our books.

© 2006 TASCHEN GmbH
Hohenzollernring 53, D-50672 Köln
**www.taschen.com**

**PROJECT MANAGEMENT:** Florian Kobler and Barbara Huttrop, Cologne
**PRODUCTION:** Thomas Grell, Cologne
**DESIGN:** Sense/Net, Andy Disl and Birgit Reber, Cologne
**GERMAN TRANSLATION:** Caroline Behlen, Berlin
**FRENCH TRANSLATION:** Jacques Bosser, Paris

Printed in Italy
ISBN-13: 978-3-8228-5260-6
ISBN-10: 3-8228-5260-0